MARCHING ON
TOGETHER

TERRACE BANTER

*For my Dad and Grandad, who both died during
the writing of this book. I miss you both.*

Marching On Together - (Pbk)

© Richard Sutcliffe, 2001

ISBN 095359209X

Published by Terrace Banter, Scotland
Printed by Heritage Press, England

The Author asserts the moral right to be identified as the author of this work.

TERRACE BANTER
P.O. Box 12, Lockerbie, Dumfriesshire. DG11 3BW. Scotland.
www.terracebanter.com

MARCHING ON
TOGETHER

Richard Sutcliffe

Introduction

I am probably the only Leeds United fan who is relieved that we didn't reach the Champions League final in 2001.

I'd seen every match of that campaign and felt as sick as everyone else when we trailed away from the Mestella Stadium after the semi-final defeat in Valencia. But for me it turned out to be a godsend. The moment I'd been dreading for nearly two years arrived 36 hours before Valencia faced Bayern Munich in the final in Milan – my Dad died.

The doctors had told us he'd got terminal cancer in September, 1999, yet somehow he'd defied the odds to keep going. But we knew it was serious when he was admitted to a hospice near our home in Keighley at midday on Monday the 21st of May with breathing difficulties. Still he kept fighting, and when I said goodbye to him that night he seemed back to his cheerful self and said, 'See you tomorrow lunchtime.'

He never made it to lunchtime. He deteriorated during the night and a nurse rang me and his brother, Peter, shortly after six the next morning. He died an hour later as we sat with him.

As I tried to come to terms with the fact that Dad was dead, I knew fate had decreed that Leeds would not reach the final so I could be with him at the end. I'd booked for Milan as soon as we'd beaten Deportivo La Coruna in the quarter finals. We'd realised that if Leeds got to the final the airfares to Northern Italy would rocket, so we decided to risk 80 quid just in case.

The flight to Genoa was scheduled for 7am on the Tuesday and we were going to travel down to Stansted shortly after midnight. I know that Dad would have insisted I went which would have meant I would have been summoned back from the airport and arrived too late, or even worse, heard of his death when I landed in Italy.

It had been a tough few months as I watched Dad gradually get weaker from Christmas onwards, and at times it was only Leeds that kept me going. Watching United with Tally, Whitby John and the rest of my mates, whether in the Premiership or on our trips round

Europe, briefly took my mind off the mixture of pain, anger and frustration that I felt the rest of the time. The run to the semi-finals kept me up when, in truth, I was feeling very down as my Dad endured more pain that anyone should have to go through. Not being able to do anything to help him hurt like hell.

Dad gave me so much, not least my love of football. From the age of five he took me to watch all manner of sports. We'd go off together to rugby league, boxing, cricket and horse racing, anticipating the event on the way, analysing it on the way home. But our passion was football.

Dad followed Burnley from the 1950s. He was there through the golden years of McIllroy and Adamson, when they were always in contention for the Championship and when they had a season ticket to at least the quarter-finals of the FA Cup. Even when they declined, at one stage almost going out of the League, he remained faithful to the Clarets and one of the last trips we shared together was to Turf Moor just three weeks before he died. Seeing Burnley beat Watford 2-0 in the final game of the season gave my Dad such a huge lift that he smiled through the pain for days afterwards. Peter and I sponsored the matchball for a Burnley home game in Dad's memory the following season. He'd have liked that.

His love of Burnley, however, didn't exclude other clubs and he liked to watch the local teams near our Keighley home, and if Burnley weren't playing he and I would satisfy our need for a football fix by travelling to Bradford, Leeds or Huddersfield. It was on one of these trips that I made my first visit to Elland Road. I was eight years old when I first sat in the West Stand to watch Leeds and West Ham share six goals. I hadn't realised it was possible to experience that much excitement.

I was hooked and pestered Dad constantly until he agreed to give up a Burnley trip to take me back for the next home game. Even a dull goalless draw against Spurs did nothing to dent my enthusiasm. That Christmas, Dad bought me my first Leeds kit, and despite the chill, I insisted on going outside to show off my yellow and blue pin-striped glory.

We still spent more time at Turf Moor than at Elland Road and I began to long for the time when I would be old enough to go to football on my own. As soon as that moment came, with the careless indifference of sons to the feelings of fathers, I chose

6

Leeds. They were my team. Dad and I settled into the comfortable banter of rival fans – he teasing me for going all the way to Moscow for a match that was frozen off, me replying by reminding him of the time he'd driven to Exeter and back for a match that never happened.

Since Dad died there have been bleak moments when it feels as though the sadness will overwhelm me. I miss him terribly and always will. At those moments I try to focus on the good times he and I had together, and also the magical experience of Leeds' Champions League adventure that helped me get through the worst time of my life.

Richard Sutcliffe
2001

Chapter One

Marvels In Munich

Any sane person hearing us singing and laughing as we clambered aboard the train at King's Cross would have assumed that Leeds United had just scored at least six goals to beat Manchester United in the Cup final. The reality was that we had just witnessed a tired, uninspired goalless draw at West Ham. But we knew it was enough to put us in the Champions League next season. We were back in the big time. Or rather we were in the big time because only a couple of us were old enough to remember the last time Leeds had played against the biggest clubs in Europe.

The chatter as we drew out of London had all the heady illogicality, pompous expertise, and boastful expectation that only true fans can produce when in a state of high excitement. Suddenly, people who only two years before had been celebrating a penalty shoot-out win over the part-timers of Maritimo as though it was the greatest victory in the club's history, were being sniffy about who they wanted to play next season. Real Madrid, AC Milan, Barcelona and Juventus were okay, but we didn't want any more of those second raters we'd put up with in the UEFA Cup. We are Leeds – the cream of Europe. That lot from Old Trafford could have the rubbish.

We'd made the transition from mid-table survivors to potential European champions with hardly a blink. As true fans, we'd always known that Leeds' place was among the greatest clubs in the world and only a gypsy's curse, UEFA bias, or unimaginative managers had held us back. That game against Maritimo had been George Graham's last in charge before he jumped ship to join Spurs because they had 'more potential', a decision that now looks as astute as that of the record company boss who turned down The Beatles.

George did some good things at Leeds, but I was glad to see him go – we wouldn't have made the progress we have under David O'Leary if he'd stayed. O'Leary may claim to be 'a young, naïve manager', but he immediately gave some good youngsters their chance, brought in good players, and above all, let the side express itself and attack. You could only take so many of George's sterile 0-0 draws and console yourself with the fact that it was another point in the bag.

Finishing third in the Premiership meant we had to qualify for the group stages of the competition, so we were hoping for an iron curtain Mickey-Mouse side to ease our way to the big boys. I slipped quietly out of the office to my car to listen to the draw. I started with Radio Five (which was far from bloody live that day), on to Talk Sport then Radio Leeds. All of them were pumping out the kind of banal garbage that has people reaching for their tapes. Don't these people realise how important this draw is?

As I frantically station hopped, my mobile rang. It was Andy from Dagenham. "We've got 1860 Munich. They were fourth in the Bundesliga and are supposed to be a bit tasty. It could have been worse, I suppose."

He didn't seem convinced. Nor was I. Admittedly as an unseeded side - more UEFA bias – we could have faced Inter Milan, Dynamo Kiev or last season's beaten finalists, Valencia. But still, how come we got one of those ruthlessly well organised German sides who are so difficult to beat? The year before Chelsea had a nice easy loosener against Latvia's finest, Skonto Riga. But those London clubs always are lucky. And Rangers, the overblown, over-expensive Champions of a third-rate league, were paired with Herfoelge, a Danish team who would provide the kind of weak opposition the Ibrox mob feed off week-in, week-out north of the border.

At least one of our usual gang, 'The Doctor', was happy with the draw. His mother, who he loves even more than Leeds United, is German so he was looking forward to visiting her homeland for the second leg. Still he's as daft as a coachload of monkeys anyway. He got his name because his hair looks like Tom Baker's in his Dr Who heyday, and he's been watching Leeds for 40 of his 47 years. There's nothing he loves more than to try and publicly embarrass his mates. I was once standing on a busy train en route to a match

10

when the Doctor walked up to me and in his foghorn voice cried, "Greetings, fellow pervert!"

Instantly, everyone in the carriage was looking at me and, try as I might to look angelic and innocent, I knew they all believed I was someone to avoid. He's pulled similar strokes on me many times, and I've still not mastered a technique for deflecting his attentions.

They tell me his brother is even dafter than he is. As he supports the team from Old Trafford and once tried to hijack a plane "for a laugh", I can believe it, and put The Doctor's eccentricity down to the bad influence he had growing up. Whatever the reason, not even the psychiatrist's couch has been able to cure him. Although he did try. After being told to see a psychiatrist a few years ago, and despite his scepticism, The Doctor vowed he would give it a go. All went well until he was handed a piece of paper and a pen and asked to draw a house.

He obliged. "What about some windows and a door, Nicholas?"

Now he knew he had a problem because only his mother called him by his given name. Still he drew some windows and door, and added a chimney for good measure.

"Who lives in the house?"

"What?"

"Who lives in the house? Is it mummy and daddy?"

The Doctor thought for a moment before saying, "I think you need more fucking help than I do, mate," and marched out, never to return.

Most of us suspected The Doctor's nostalgic visit to the land of his mother might be the only good thing to come out of this European campaign. Years of watching your side through thin and thin does tend to make you err towards the pessimistic. The fact that the first leg at Elland Road was ten days before the Premiership season kicked off, and we were going to be without Harry Kewell, Jonathan Woodgate, Jason Wilcox and Stephen McPhail through injury, didn't ease the gloom.

The good news, to which we clung with dogged persistence, was that David O'Leary had splashed out £13million on Olivier Dacourt from Lens and Mark Viduka from Celtic to strengthen the squad. Dacourt had impressed me during his one season at Everton, although his disciplinary record suggested he might not play a full season – he'd been booked in every one of his first nine games in

English football. I was less sure about Viduka. Admittedly he'd scored 27 goals in his season at Celtic and been voted Scotland's Player of the Year, but as Andy succinctly put it, "I'd fancy my own chances of scoring 27 goals against the defenders they've got up there."

There's nothing quite like the first game of the season. With the relief that the long, boring summer is finally over, even the beer tastes different. Yorkshire had again teased us into hoping they would win the County Championship for the first time since before man walked on the moon, only to belly flop like Devon Loch on the final run-in. We would have to wait another 12 months for the Championship to come 'home'. Apart from that it had been the usual arid spell: nothing on TV, papers full of crap and wild speculation that you knew in your gut couldn't be true, and the continual anti-climax of punching up Ceefax just in case Leeds had made another signing. It's enough to make you contemplate marriage.

I arranged to meet Andy, who, as ever, travelled up from Essex to watch the lads. This game was a bonus for him. He usually missed out on midweek fixtures because he works shifts, but his works plant close down for two weeks in August so he was able make it. We spent the afternoon in a pilgrimage to our usual haunts – O'Reilly's, Spencer's, the Prince of Wales, and The Conservatory. I was kidding Andy because he'd been arrested the previous March for the heinous crime of jumping on the cinder track behind the net at Bradford City when Michael Bridges made it 2-0. He'd been fined £240 plus costs, but, all importantly, had not been given a banning order. The press cutting of his case, which describes him as a "loyal fan who spends all is money on watching Leeds United" is one of his proudest possessions.

As we wandered from pub to pub we kept bumping into people we hadn't seen since May and everyone you met asked, "How are you getting to Munich?"

We also came across several German fans taking in the delights of our 24 hour city. That wouldn't have been possible on match day in the 1970s and 1980s when even people from Huddersfield were viewed as 'foreigners', and few visiting fans would be suicidal enough to drink in pubs near the railway station. But these days Leeds is a much more welcoming place with only the annual visit of that lot from Manchester resulting in the pubs being closed and what feels like the massed ranks of the whole West Yorkshire police force finding their way to the streets.

But here, on an brilliant sunny day, German and English fans drank and chatted in the same bars, each keeping up the pretence of confidence their side would come out on top, while worrying that the other side looked as though they believed what they were saying. But if you can't believe it's going to be a special season on the day of the first match, when the hell can you?

As always the police spotters were out, monitoring the fans, trying to pick out known troublemakers. The relationship between football supporters and the police is often uneasy simply because a large number of fans, who have no intention of causing trouble or fighting, find many of the restrictions imposed on them unnecessarily petty. We just want to have a good day out, supporting our team, having a few drinks and a laugh. All football fans are not hooligans looking for a fight and to wreck anything, and most of the behaviour that gets criticised in football fans is passed off as high spirits when it happens at university balls or rugby union dinners. Sometimes we can't resist taking the piss and Watford in 1999 was one of Leeds fans' best efforts.

As we came out of the station, Watford seemed to be on red alert with pubs closed and a large police presence in the town centre. Five burly policemen stood eyeing the Leeds faithful as they left the station and a plot was quickly hatched. A group of fans suddenly raced off up the road as though something had kicked off with the home fans. Once round the corner they hid behind a wall for the five breathless officers to come past, then jumped out and shouted, "Surprise! Now it's your turn to hide. We'll count to ten and find you!"

At least the coppers had the grace to laugh. That's how it should be.

I suppose this summer had been shorter than most what with Euro 2000 and early start to the campaign, but it still seemed a hell of a long time since I'd seen those reassuring words 'Leeds United' emblazoned across the back of the East Stand. That had been for a 1-1 draw with Everton in the Premiership that was followed by a half-hearted lap of honour. Six days later we got the point we needed to qualify for the Champions League and celebrated long into the night.

That first glimpse of the stadium as the bus pulls off the M621 ups the pace of the pulse, and the anticipation as you climb the steps of the Kop for the first game is like that moment on a first date when you think, *Bingo! I'm in here.*

I'd been to Huddersfield and Blackburn for pre-season games just to get some football, but as always, those matches were a let down. You try to be interested, to see what the new signings are like, check out who is in for a big season, but you know deep down, it's all meaningless. But this was different. This was the start of a Champions League campaign. I didn't dare hope too much, but neither could I contemplate going out before we'd even reached the group stage. I'd settle for the first group stage. That would be a good achievement at our first attempt. I just hoped the players weren't feeling as nervous as I was.

The team was announced with Alan Smith joining Mark Viduka and Michael Bridges in a three man attack. Brave tactics, but what if they left us exposed at the back? We didn't want to be trailing when we went to Bavaria for the second leg. We tried to reassure each other over the noise of the inane chatter from the announcer.

It's generally agreed that Smithy is the natural heir to David Batty as the Leeds fans' favourite son. He talks like us and seems to be the kind of bloke who would be on the Kop with us if he weren't the feistiest centre forward since Allan Clarke. He'd not played very well by his own standards last season, failing to live up to the amazing breakthrough he'd made when he scored with his first touch at Anfield the year before.

He'd followed that up by netting in the next game against Charlton. This time it was his second touch, prompting someone to yell from the Kop, "Your standards are slipping, Smith. Pull yourself together, lad!"

We all hoped the arrival of Mark Viduka, giving Leeds a genuine target man for the first time since Lee Chapman, would allow Smithy to get back to doing what he does best, scoring goals.

I was expecting a cauldron of noise to greet the players, willing them on to qualification. Instead it was not much more than warm applause. There was a half-hearted rendition of 'We are Leeds!' followed by the obligatory 'Stand up if you hate Man U!'. But everyone was soon seated again and the atmosphere was alarmingly muted. There were empty seats dotted around Elland Road – clearly some fans were still on holiday, and obviously it must have been the noisiest ones who were basking on beaches around Europe. We were being outshouted by about 2,000 German fans in the South Stand. It didn't feel right.

Fortunately Smithy dragged us out of our slumbers when he nipped in to flick a weak back-header into the net, and by the time Ian Harte rolled in a second half penalty, we were back in full voice. This was okay. A two goal lead for the second leg would be plenty. This German team wasn't as invincible as we'd feared.

We'd reckoned without the intervention of Costas Kapitanis, a fussy referee from Cyprus. He'd already somewhat harshly sent off 1860's Ned Zelic, and 15 minutes from time he struck again. This time it was Olly Dacourt. The Frenchman appeared to be tripped as he raced down the middle towards the Kop, but Mr Kapitanis saw it as a dive and sent him off for a second bookable offence. Six minutes from time, he struck again, this time sending off Eirik Bakke.

Beside me, Andy was clearly unhappy. "Cheating bastard!" was the kindest remark he yelled at the official, who then sent my Essex mate apoplectic by adding four minutes stoppage time. Sure enough, 1860 took full advantage and with virtually the last kick of the game Paul Agostino thumped the ball past Nigel Martyn. They had the away goal. A 1-0 win in Germany would see them through. Their fans were delirious. I stood there feeling as though someone had kicked me in the balls. I felt sick. I felt angry. I felt completely frustrated.

As we made our way back to the centre of town, talk turned to the inevitability of a 'bent' referee robbing us against a Munich side. "Look at the way that French fucker robbed us in the '75 European Cup final," somebody said, referring to the 2-0 defeat by Bayern Munich when Peter Lorimer had a perfectly good goal disallowed and Leeds had a blatant penalty turned down. That official never took charge of another game and the general opinion was that Mr Kapitanis should be treated the same way. "He's probably cost us a place in the next round. We'll end up back in the UEFA Cup thanks to him."

As Andy and I waited for our trains, too downbeat to bother with more than a pint, we wondered what our midfield would be for the second leg. Dacourt and Bakke would be suspended, Kewell, McPhail and Wilcox were still injured. That left Lee Bowyer. He's a great player but single handed . . . well, it didn't fire me with confidence.

I'd only started a new job six weeks before, so decided it would be a bit cheeky to ask for three days off already. Instead I opted for the club's one day trip. Leaving Leeds-Bradford at nine in the morning and arriving back in the early hours of the next day was a gruelling prospect, but I reasoned it might be our only Champions League trip of the season so I had to be there. My mates flew out the day before the match. They went in via Frankfurt and caught a connecting coach to Munich. I felt several pangs of jealousy as I phoned to wish them a good trip and arrange to meet up in Munich.

I was anxious because someone told me that in Moscow the previous year, those on the day trip had only been given their match tickets when they got on the coach to the stadium. I didn't want that because I was planning to go to the match with my mates and certainly didn't fancy being escorted through the streets by the police and having to sit in the stadium for an hour ahead of kick-off. Luckily the match ticket was with the travel documents handed out at Leeds-Bradford.

I'd arranged to meet the lads near the Hauptbahnhof at one o'clock. As usual I heard The Doctor before I saw him. When eventually he came round the corner, his jeans were soaking wet from running through a fountain 'for a laugh'. Munich was made for football fans. Situated in the south west of Germany, it's the capital of the Bavarian region and renowned for its Bier Kellers and the capacity of its residents. They each sup an average of 350 litres of beer a year – 100 litres more than in the rest of Germany. And as there are bound to be some tee-totallers (there are sad bastards all round the world), some of them must be getting on for 400 litres each. Munich is where you go to find the German stereotype of a beer-belching, sausage-eating, Lederhosen-clad native with a beard. And that's just the women!

Of course, most stereotypes are rubbish. After all, London fans still insist on whistling the tune from the Hovis advert at us, yet I can't remember the last time I saw a whippet or a flat cap at Elland

Road. But Munich was the exception, and we had our photo taken with a strapping lad in Lederhosen just because we didn't think people back at home would believe he existed.

I could tell the lads had enjoyed a good night because Keith looked like death, slightly warmed up. He's known as 'Bleugh' because he tends to throw up during and after heavy drinking sessions. His trips always follow the same pattern. He's fine the first day, but by the second morning he's feeling so rough he can't sup any more beer for the rest of the trip. Instead he opts for vodka and coke which just gets him drunk quicker. We've discussed pacing himself better, but he doesn't seem to understand the term. By the time I met up with them, he was a mess and quietly followed us round the sights, taking in a vodka every time we stopped for fuel. Fortunately the main points of interest in Munich are quite close together and we were able to settle in a market square with four or five beer gardens dotted around the edge, the ideal place to spend an afternoon in the sun as we waited for the match.

We started talking to an elderly German couple. The woman, who must have been in her seventies, said, "Are you here to fight? We watched the fighting between England and German fans in Belgium on television. Were you there?"

We assured her we preferred to watch Leeds than England and had spent our money going to places like Moscow and the Czech Republic last season.

"Ach, so you are good boys. Those English boys in Belgium could not hold their beer."

While we had been talking, her husband had gone to the bar and returned with a couple of huge glasses, holding about three pints of lager each. We had been supping gracefully at modest pints, but were soon persuaded to switch to a *Stein*. I found it hard enough just to hold the bloody thing and we hardened northern drinkers soon found ourselves outdrunk by a German granny.

As afternoon merged into evening we decided to move closer to the Olympic Stadium. We hailed a taxi and said, "Take us to the finest bar in Munich." Something must have been lost in the translation because he dropped us off at a go-kart track. We didn't really feel up to racing around the track so we had a couple more beers in the fumes of the go-kart arena, one of the stranger venues for a pre-match bevvy.

The talk turned to the match and how much we were looking forward to the Olympic Stadium. Our UEFA Cup excursions had taken us to some of the more primitive venues on the European circuit. Slavia Prague's Strahov Stadium was very basic with crumbling terraces reminding me of Halifax's Shay in the mid 1980s. Prague was a magnificent city, probably my favourite in Europe, but the tatty national stadium didn't live up to the rest of the place. However compared to Lokomotiv Moscow's home, the Strahov was positively palatial.

To get to the toilet at half time, I had to come out of the away fans' section and walk right round the stadium to the Lokomotiv end. It wasn't a comfortable experience. I was standing letting nature take its course when all hell broke out a few cubicles down. Within seconds the Russian riot police charged in. I tried to be invisible, hoping I wouldn't get caught up in some all too typical 'crack English skulls, ask questions later' police methods. Fortunately for the Leeds fans in the toilet, the poor English guy under attack had his eye gashed open, so the police could see who the wronged party was and arrested the three locals who had jumped him from the rear as he had a piss. When you consider how basic the facilities are there, and the record of clubs like Galatasaray in Istanbul, you wonder how UEFA continue to grant these stadiums a licence.

There are no such doubts about Munich's showpiece stadium, built for the 1972 Olympic Games and host to memorable moments like Germany's '74 World Cup triumph, Holland's victory in the 1988 European Championships, and Nottingham Forest's European Cup triumph over Malmo in 1979. It's simply magnificent with a spectacular spider-web glass roof extending over the main stand and part of the north and south stands.

We walked through a park to the main turnstiles for the away fans. There was a massive police presence which seemed a bit futile once we'd got in because we found ourselves on the unsegregated concourse running round the top of the steep banks of seats with German and English fans mingling freely. The 1860 fans were an amiable bunch although their persistent predictions of a home win soon began to get on my nerves. Okay, so one of them thought they'd win 2-0, and another thought 3-0, "though 1-0 will do", but when you've heard it for the 20th time, it begins to grate.

The problem was of course that we weren't feeling entirely confident that our lads could do enough to get through and the last thing we needed was our fragile belief being undermined. It's funny the little things that creep into your brain and sew little seeds of doubt. Would the fact that the 1860 players were said to be on £10,000 a man to get through make a difference? No, we told ourselves, this wasn't about cash. But the worm kept gnawing away.

We knew we had selection problems. Matthew Jones was pressed into action despite only completing one training session since recovering from injury. Lucas Radebe was pushed forward to midfield. David O'Leary had no choice. No wonder he called on his players to "play the game of your lives".

The 700 or so Leeds fans were stretched out across one section of the south stand, looking a little exposed and frail compared to the 55,000 home support, about 20,000 higher than their average crowd. The oom-pah band was amplified through the speakers, but we were defiant and determined to make our voices heard:

"Marching On Together. We're gonna see you win,
Na na na na na na,
We are so proud. We shout it out loud,
We love you, Leeds! Leeds! Leeds!"

Seven hundred people, most of them unknown to each other, but for that moment united as one family, wanting to let those figures down there on the pitch know they were not alone. Nigel Martyn turned and applauded us. We knew we could be heard.

At half-time, still goalless, Andy said what we were all hoping but dare not voice aloud. "If we can score early in the second half, we're through. They'll never come back from that."

He should have done the lottery that week because inside a minute of the restart, Viduka seized the ball on the right of the penalty area, 1860 hesitated just long enough for him to roll it to Smith who had the icy nerve to steady himself before slipping it past the keeper. Cue pandemonium! We sang, we danced, we punched the air, we jumped up and down, we hugged complete strangers as though they were long lost family. I didn't know 700 people could make so much noise.

As if conducted by some invisible figure, everyone launched into a passionate rendering of "We're all going on a European tour!"

19

This was how I had imagined Champions League football would be – great stadiums, good opponents and Leeds winning.

At the end of the game the team came to salute us. We applauded them. They had been magnificent. I know I was not alone in hoping we would go through but fearing that the injuries and suspensions would cost us against a very good German side. But once again David O'Leary's young side had shown we were wrong to doubt them and their resilience.

I said my goodbye to The Doctor and the rest of the lads as they headed into the city centre to celebrate. I arrived back in Keighley at three in the morning, completely knackered but still pumped up enough to put the video on and watch the winning goal about 50 times before dragging myself off to bed for a few hours sleep before going to work. At last I could allow myself to dream about watching Leeds against the biggest sides in Europe.

Chapter Two

The Pain In Spain

As I waited for the group stage draw, the main prize in my mind was Barcelona. I'd clung to the ambition of watching the Mighty Whites in the Nou Camp for as long as I could remember. I don't know why, after all the last time we'd played them – a second-leg 1-1 draw putting us into the 1975 European Cup final – I was just about to celebrate my second birthday. Perhaps it was because I'd missed out on the match in the Nou Camp when we'd stuck two fingers up to UEFA by beating Stuttgart in a re-arranged European Cup tie in 1992.

The Germans had played too many foreigners in the match at Elland Road and instead of throwing them out and sending United through, UEFA ordered a rematch as far away from Leeds as they could manage. Thankfully, Carl Shutt grabbed his place among the immortals by scoring the winner a minute after coming off the subs bench. I'd just started at college in London and hadn't been able to go to Spain and had listened enviously as my mates told triumphant tales of being one of the 'few' to make the trip.

As it turned out the draw was better than we could have hoped for. We knew Besiktas and the return to Istanbul, the city where two fans had been murdered just the year before, would be emotional and highly charged. But to get Barcelona and AC Milan in our group was like being in a lottery winning syndicate and finding you were the only one who'd paid your dues.

Immediately the mobiles were red hot with calls and text messages, sorting out travel options. Unfortunately, we weren't quick enough to beat the sharks in the travel companies – within minutes the cost of a flight to Barcelona shot up from £100 to £300. To avoid being ripped off you have to be a bit ingenious (and willing to put up with a little discomfort). We ended up flying into Carcassonne in the south of France, then sitting on a train to Barcelona for four hours. It was a bum-numbing trip, but we were all on tight budgets so had little option. Anyway we knew it would be a laugh with our lot.

The most important thing about these long trips is to choose your company very carefully. One pain in the arse can wreck it for everyone. I like to travel with lads who like a beer, enjoy a laugh and, above all, love Leeds United. Over the years I've made some great mates and I set off to Spain with four of them – Alec, Spam, Whitby John and Tally.

With the sparkling wit we football fans are notorious for, John gets his name because he lives in Whitby. He makes most football fans look like part-timers – he's not missed a Leeds match since the opening day of the 1982-83 season and early in 2002 is set to chalk up his 1,000th consecutive competitive game. This doesn't include all the pre-season friendlies he's been to round the world. He went to Japan when Howard Wilkinson's team were invited to play in Tokyo, but whereas most people would have stayed to do a bit of sight-seeing, John flew straight back so he wouldn't miss a West Riding Cup tie against Halifax. This being Leeds, especially Wilko's post-title winning Leeds, his reward for rushing home was a 2-0 defeat.

John organises our trips and you can sometimes see him during the build up to a match, ticking the names off his list and stuffing the cash in his pocket. On a busy day he can get quite distracted, looking over his shoulder in case anyone realises he's got three grand on him. We'd heard rumours that Leeds United were only going to sell match tickets to people booking through their travel company, but like so many of the conspiracy theories that sweep around the terraces as rapidly as Man United change strips, this proved to be a load of bollocks. In fact we didn't have a problem all season – once we'd produced our itinerary, passports and away card membership numbers, the tickets always plopped through the letterbox. But with the seed of doubt planted, I still greeted them with as much relief as excitement.

The time between the draw and setting off seemed like an eternity. The team had started the season quite well, but then they'd been beaten at home by Manchester City and only managed a drab goalless draw against Coventry. We tried to put out of our minds the obvious thought that if we couldn't beat two of the worst sides in the Premiership, how the hell would we do against Rivaldo and Co?

With expectation born of nothing more than blind loyalty and mindless optimism we finally set off. It was an unremarkable trip until our train stopped at Perpignon where about 50 Leeds fans climbed on board. They included Pop and his wife, Michelle. Pop is someone Tally has known since their schooldays and is also known to us as 'Loose Cannon' or 'Ten Men', the latter a result of a charge to clear a group of German fans from a spot behind the goal during Leeds match against Stuttgart. This led one awestruck Leeds fan remarking to Tally, "Look at your mate, he's worth ten men."

As he joined us he immediately started to wind up Tally and Keith. "Bloody Leeds fans, you must be joking!" he said, before turning to me and adding, "I was at school with them and when they were snotty nosed kids. One supported Doncaster bloody Rovers and the other Nottingham Forest. They're just jumping on the bandwagon!"

After a bit more banter we got back to the serious drinking before Pop came close to causing an international incident. As the Spanish police boarded the train to check our passports, Alec leaned over to Pop and said, "See if he'll let you look at his gun?"

Pop thought this was a great idea, leaned over and tried to take the gun out of its holster. Needless to say, the four policemen in the buffet weren't too impressed, but they let him off with a warning.

Barcelona is a great city. I'm not the most enthusiastic sight-seer in the world and have some sympathy with the West Brom player who preferred to play cards rather than take a trip to the Great Wall of China, a moment immortalised with his excuse, "When you've seen one wall, you've seen 'em all."

But there is definitely a special atmosphere in the Catalan capital that grabs you as soon as you step off the train. Like millions before us, we made our way to Las Ramblas, the main tree-lined thoroughfare running from the centre of the city down to the sea, where you can buy anything from flowers to parrots, chickens and rabbits. The traffic is restricted to two narrow streets on either side so the pedestrian is king and day or night there always seems something new to look at. I was particularly taken with the street artists who pose as statues, moving only when someone gives them money. It really is difficult to tell that they are indeed flesh and

23

blood and not stone. They make the Buckingham Palace guardsmen look as though they've got the shakes

Las Ramblas was soon awash with Leeds fans and the atmosphere was light-hearted and not at all menacing. I find it so much more enjoyable travelling to watch Leeds than England. We all like a drink, but when you look at the state of some England fans you wonder if they can remember their own names never mind the players'. The Leeds support seems to be a bit older and more intent on having a good time whereas the England support adopt a siege mentality and seem to need to prove how macho they are. Trouble does occur from time to time on Leeds trips, but mostly we tend to be the targets rather than the aggressors. There certainly haven't been any large scale outbreaks of violence like those seen in both France 98 and Euro 2000.

The trouble is the fighting in Marseilles and Charleroi, which was seen all over the world, colours people's view of all English football fans, and places where we used to be greeted with open arms as a source of additional income now make us about as welcome as Saddam Hussein in the White House. Practically every trip with Leeds was greeted in the local paper by warnings about 'hooligans' only to be followed up after the game with a 'shock' story that there hadn't been any problems.

Our group had arrived in Barcelona without bothering to book in for the night and ended up having to split up to find rooms. I went off with Tally to see what we could find. He and I have been mates for years and he's great to have along because he can always find a bar where we can get a drink whatever time it is. He has a theory of following the local drunks because they will lead you to the right places that serve ale regardless of the licensing laws. He and I have had some massive sessions over the years, one of the best being in Newcastle. The two of us had stopped off for a 'quick one' while we waited for our train connection to take us to Sunderland for a match. We got chatting to some Newcastle fans who decided to take us on a pub crawl of the city centre. Some time later, as we stretched out on a pub floor singing, 'Lie down if you hate Sunderland!', we suddenly remembered the match.

We arrived at the Stadium of Light just before half-time. I can't remember much about it, but the papers the next day said Leeds won 2-1, so it must have been good.

Tally and I found a nice room just off Las Ramblas, but when we met up with the others again, they felt their accommodation fell a little short of the Ritz. It didn't really matter though because we didn't intend to spend much time sleeping anyway. We bumped into loads of Leeds fans, many of who had found ingenious ways of getting to Barcelona cheaper than the direct route. Their journeys had taken them via Malaga, Madrid and even Bilbao, but all agreed Barcelona was a bit special.

Of course every silver lining has a cloud, and in the Catalan capital it's pickpockets. Almost everyone you met had a horror story they'd heard about people losing money, wallets, purses and handbags. Being a Yorkshireman, I tend to protect my cash vigilantly, and I became extra cautious as I heard more and more tales of woe. The biggest culprits are the whores. They make amorous advances on some unsuspecting punter and while he is getting excited about the prospects for his family jewels, they nick most of his other valuables. We spotted one go to work on a poor Leeds fan, slipping his wallet out of his back pocket as she stuck her tongue down his throat, but fortunately our shouts alerted him, and when we started to crowd round she threw it back at him and went off to find a less protected victim.

Some of the Barcelona thieves proved better at it than she was and by morning our group had 'lost' a gold chain, a bracelet, two passports and around a hundred quid in cash, while Pop and Michelle had their passports stolen from their rooms. We traipsed off to report it to the police so we could make an insurance claim and they told us they had issued 300 theft notices from just one police station on Las Ramblas that night.

The day of the game always brings with it a thrill in the air as the anticipation and excitement build gradually ahead of kick-off.

With the hotel we had found the previous night being full it meant we needed another bed for the night. Unfortunately, everywhere brought the same response. "Sorry, sir. We are booked up for the whole week."

We knew this was rubbish. We were even leaving one hotel when an American marched in with his wife, and despite the reception telling us just ten seconds earlier that it was full, a double room had miraculously become available. But what can you do? After about half an hour of knockbacks, and feeling like Joseph and

25

Mary must have done in Bethlehem, we decided to dump our bags in left luggage at the train station and take our chances. All we were bothered about was the match and certainly didn't want to waste time traipsing round a city looking for an elusive bed.

Las Ramblas was the place to be that afternoon as the temperature crept up towards 80 degrees. Sight-seeing was not on the agenda so the art museums which house the works of Picasso and Antoni Tapies would have to wait. Instead, we took the chance to top up our tans while drinking and watching the world pass by.

Drinking is as much a part of the British culture as fish and chips. Even the most intelligent of people can't wait to tell you how many pints they had the previous night and how they had been "paralytic". It is just how we Brits are. The late American comedian, Bill Hicks, once said, "You Brits drink as though someone is going to take it away from you." I couldn't agree more.

Moving between the pavement cafes was a pleasant way of passing the afternoon. Unlike some trips, there was no threat or menace in the air from the locals and we didn't see many home fans until we reached the stadium. The most common comment was, "It's not like a football trip. It is more like being in Ibiza for the week."

We were all in high spirits and eagerly looking forward to the game, although Brighton John, who is the spitting image of EastEnders' character Billy Mitchell, didn't look in the best of health when we bumped into him just off Las Ramblas. One side of his body was covered in black bruises and I initially thought he must have been knocked down by a car.

"I was a bit the worse for wear last night and ended up jumping off a train when we were pulling out of one of the stations. One of the lads had got off with my bag thinking I was behind him, but I was still on the train. I saw him through the window and the train had started to pull away."

"Why didn't you just stay on until the next stop?" I asked.

"I thought I could make it but didn't realise the train was moving so fast. I jumped and the next thing I knew the pain was unbearable all down my left side. I had to have a few drinks last night to dull the pain but it is killing me again now."

"If I were you I would get that looked at by the hospital. You could have done yourself a serious injury."

"No chance." He was adamant. "They might keep me in and then I'd miss the game. I'm not risking that."

As it turned out, he had a check-up when he got back to England and the doctor said he was lucky because he had only suffered bruising and no internal injuries.

Most Leeds fans had bought tickets before leaving England although there were a few who had travelled in the hope of paying in on the day. We were approached by a couple of lads asking if anyone had any spares. We didn't have any, but the word was they were readily available from the ground. In the end, they paid £30 for the best seats in the house while we paid a fiver less in Leeds but ended up sat 200 feet above the Nou Camp pitch.

As the day wore on, we gradually started to move up Las Ramblas to catch the Metro to the Nou Camp and, hopefully, a famous victory.

That week's Spanish newspapers had warned its readers of the impending invasion by thousands of Leeds 'hooligans' who, it claimed, would all go on the rampage the moment they arrived. The following day's newspaper headlines told a different story, however, all being a variation of the 'no hooligans here' theme. They were invariably accompanied by photos of Leeds fans posing with Las Ramblas' famous human statues. One article went on to say, in a rather incredulous tone, that 'the Leeds fans were just like tourists as they soaked up the sun and enjoyed a few drinks. They will be welcome here again.'

We had enjoyed the day of sun in the Catalan capital, but knew why we were here. We were going to face one of world football's biggest names, and, hopefully, come away with a point or even all three.

The people of Barcelona are rightly proud of their team. They do not view themselves as Spanish and the official language is Catalan. As recently as 1975, their own language was outlawed and it was only the death of the Spanish dictator, General Franco, which ended this outrageous practice. The Catalans rightly see FC Barcelona as the flag-bearer for their region and culture. Any victory over Real Madrid - Franco's favoured team - prompts joyous scenes across the whole region.

Surprisingly for such a major club, Barcelona have just one European Cup to their name, won in 1992 with victory over

Sampdoria at Wembley. In contrast, Real Madrid's triumph in Paris in May 2000 was their eighth and this clearly rankles with the Catalans. It is a city in which everyone seems to care passionately about their team - taxi drivers, bar owners, hotel receptionists, even, I guess, the pickpockets.

Countless locals, who weren't even going to the game, politely told us it was their year for lifting the Champions League. We were just glad to be taking part in the competition for the first time and although we secretly hoped for a win, we agreed a good performance would do to set us up for the forthcoming home clashes with AC Milan and Besiktas.

"We're Leeds and we're proud of it!" boomed around the metro train as we made our way to Maria Critina station. Emerging into the warm evening air, we were met by the sight of hundreds of Leeds fans, savouring the moment with flags adorning every shop front. The flag of St George has really made a comeback in the past couple of years at the expense of the Union Jack, which is how it should be. However, the best Leeds flag we saw all day was a huge effort with the words 'Champions of Europe' emblazoned right across it. Well, we thought, we can but dream.

The chant of "Marching On Together!" started up as we enjoyed one last drink before walking to the ground and some of the Spaniards started looking nervous. They needn't have worried because everyone was in a happy mood. There was no menace, just excitement, as we looked forward to our team taking on the likes of Rivaldo, Kluivert and Gerard.

From the outside, the stadium looked every bit as impressive as it did on television. The Nou Camp was redeveloped in the 1970s, so fans entering at ground level are actually at the back of the first tier because the pitch was lowered to accommodate thousands more seats. Once we got inside, however, it wasn't as impressive as I hoped it would be.

Yes, it is huge and there is no track around the pitch, something I do like about Spanish football grounds compared to those in Italy and Germany. It may also be Europe's largest football arena with huge steep banks of seating which make an awesome sight when full. But the facilities inside the stadium were very basic and the view from the visiting fans' seats was dreadful.

I stood with Tally and Whitby John on the back row of the third tier behind the goal, which meant we were so high that I wondered if oxygen was available under the seats. The pitch was so far away I couldn't gauge distances or follow the game, although that may have been the effect of a full day's drinking. Bearing in mind how the game went, maybe this was a bonus.

There were around 1,700 Leeds fans in our enclosure with a similar number at the other end of the vast stadium. We tried our best to offer our support, but I doubt the noise even reached the pitch with us being so high and having no roof above us.

We knew Leeds had to show Barcelona in the opening minutes that we would not be overawed and initially the signs were good. Alan Smith clattered Rivaldo in the second minute to show we meant business, and after the Brazilian received extensive treatment, Olivier Dacourt whacked him as well for good measure. We grinned at each other and started another chorus of "We are Leeds!"

Gradually, however, it became clear we were paying Barcelona far too much respect and they went ahead in the tenth minute through Rivaldo. Frank De Boer curled a 25 yard free-kick past Nigel Martyn a short while later and at 2-0 down, with not even 20 minutes on the clock, it looked like being a long night.

Alec had travelled to the stadium with us and his ticket was for the seat next to me. Somehow, he ended up sat with the home fans in the main stand on the side of the pitch. He is a season ticket holder in the Kop although he often spends most of the game watching it on television in the bar. Once, he arrived in the bar underneath the Kop at 2.30pm, remained there drinking throughout the game before catching the bus back to the city centre at 5pm.

Even though he doesn't know how he got into the home seats, Alec can recall the Spanish fans laughing at him after yet another simple pass by Leeds went astray.

"You are not very good. We like Manchester but you are a poor team."

"It will be a different story back in Leeds. We'll thrash you in the return."

Alec didn't really believe what he had said but felt he had to say something. His new Spanish 'friends' just fell about laughing - thankfully for us, Alec and Leeds did, indeed, have the last laugh.

The half-time break saw the ritual chant of "We are the Champions, Champions of Europe!" being sung while we waved our shirts above our heads. Fans of other clubs may say the time to sing such a song is not when you are 2-0 down and on course for a thrashing in Barcelona. But the fact is we sang it when we were struggling in the old Second Division so we will certainly not stop now when we are back in the big time, even if it did look like we were out of our depth in the Nou Camp.

Patrick Kluivert made it 3-0 after about 75 minutes and all I wanted was for the game to end. No such luck though as Kluivert made it 4-0 with five minutes to go.

We had seen enough and got up to leave. The last thing we wanted was to sit in the stadium for another 30 minutes after the final whistle. The police were not too keen on us leaving, but we simply ignored them. We needed a drink.

Once outside, I wanted to put as much distance between me and the stadium as possible. We walked away in silence as thousands of Spaniards celebrated a perfect start to their Champions League campaign. Two fans on a scooter tried to taunt us, with one throwing a bottle which flew inches past my head before crashing against a bus. But I just didn't care. I merely carried on walking and walking and walking. None of us said a word until eventually we realised we were well and truly lost.

"Where the hell are we? There's no-one about."

We had been deep in our own thoughts and misery, and none of us knew how we ended up here. Just ten minutes earlier, we had been surrounded by thousands of celebrating Barca fans, but now there was just silence and empty streets. In the distance was a 'Bar' sign so we headed for that. The owner turned out to be a Real Madrid supporter - I bet he doesn't advertise that fact on a matchday. He sympathised with three crest-fallen Leeds fans and just poured some cold beers.

We were in need of a lift and Tally provided it with his assessment of our rather heavy defeat. "Thank God we don't have to win the second leg 5-0 to stay in this bloody competition."

It had been a sobering experience because we weren't just beaten, we were destroyed by a team who looked far better than anything we had faced before. It had been a giant step up from the UEFA Cup.

As if being thrashed wasn't bad enough, we also heard Manchester United had beaten Anderlecht 5-1 at Old Trafford with Andy Cole scoring a hat-trick. We now faced the prospect of a night in Barcelona with no hotel room, but as we ordered another beer, the mood started to lighten.

"We play AC Milan next. I'd settle for us winning a corner, never mind the match."

"I wonder if the bookies will take a bet on the time we first cross the halfway line. I'll go for 67 minutes."

It was the sort of black humour all football fans can empathise with. We love the club and we will defend the players to the hilt against anyone who criticises them. But this was our way of dealing with such a heavy defeat. It worked. Within half an hour - and a few more beers later - it was as if the defeat had never happened. The bar owner called a taxi for us and ten minutes later we were back on Las Ramblas.

It was a balmy evening so we sat down and ordered a beer as the Leeds fans started to drift back. It was nearly midnight, but the weather was thankfully still warm so the lack of a bed didn't bother us. Our train back to France didn't leave until 8.45 the following morning so we decided to find a bar and rely on it staying open until dawn. One of the strip bars at the bottom of Las Ramblas seemed our best option.

We paid our entrance money and got talking to the owner who said he would be open until about sixish. That was perfect and, of course, we had the entertainment on stage to keep us amused. The bar owner had watched the game and said he thought we were outclassed. We certainly didn't disagree - and even if we had, we needed him to stay open so wouldn't be arguing.

A group of Leeds fans wearing sombreros came in a couple of hours after us and they ended up giving us more entertainment than the girls. They were all the worse for wear although not in an aggressive way. These lads had only been in the club three minutes when one of them leapt up on stage, startling the girl who was down to her G-string. Unfortunately, he slipped and went flying over the back of the stage. This didn't deter him though and having been returned to his seat by the manager, he tried to do exactly the same thing again. Unfortunately, this time he couldn't even jump on to the stage and landed flat on his back. We all fell about laughing,

31

but the manager was not as amused and threatened him with a chair if he did not leave. He and his mates left quietly. We were a bit worried it might affect our chances of staying all night but the owner just said, "You boys are good and you can stay until we close."

In the end, we left about half past six and decided on one last weary stroll up Las Ramblas before making our way to the station.

We stopped and talked to a couple of Leeds fans who had met John Hendrie the previous night and could hardly contain their excitement. We could hardly contain our indifference. We were knackered and just wanted to get on a train and set off home.

At the station we chatted to another group bound for Toulouse, who asked us what we thought about the terrible news about Lucas Radebe.

"What do you mean? We left five minutes before the end."

"He has broken his neck and will probably never play again. He landed really badly after a collision with Duberry in the last minute."

I couldn't believe it. Our best defender forced to retire. The 4-0 defeat was nothing compared to this. What a nightmare. They seemed so certain that we had no reason to doubt the news. One of them said it had been confirmed in a phone call home. As it turned out, the Leeds captain was not as badly injured as first feared and was able to return to the side at Derby just ten days later.

But the 'news' about Lucas meant we were a subdued bunch as the train, thankfully on time, set off back to France where we were going to catch our return flight to Stansted. I eventually got home 72 hours after setting off from Keighley and feeling like I needed a week's holiday to recover.

The result had been a nightmare, but in true football fan's style, we all agreed it had been another cracking trip. All we wanted now was for the players to somehow bounce back from such a crushing blow in just six days to give another of Europe's biggest names, AC Milan, a game at Elland Road. We would not be disappointed.

Chapter Three

Leeds Hit The Top

We've all made sacrifices to watch football. Following Leeds at home and abroad has seen me spend a lot of time and money, but I do it because I love it. I've been spat at, abused, and even been beaten up once at Tottenham, but I'll never stop following the club. I love them so much I have 'Leeds United' tattooed across my left arm.

Most of the Leeds fans I know feel the same. One of those is an old mate Paul who I bump into from time to time at Elland Road. I saw him again on the afternoon of AC Milan's visit. He looked a bit down so I asked what was bothering him.

"I lost my job last week."

"I'm sorry to hear that, mate. What happened? Were you made redundant?"

"No, I went in to work last Friday after getting back from Barcelona and the boss called me in to his office and said I was out."

I was just about to ask why when Paul spoke again.

"I couldn't get time off for Barcelona so I rang work to say I was ill on the Tuesday morning before flying to Spain. They even sounded concerned when I said I was in bed with diarrhoea. Everything was going fine until my bastard of a boss sat down to watch the game on ITV. Just my luck, the camera focused on me and my mate looking pissed off when we were 3-0 down. How unlucky is that?"

I couldn't answer as I collapsed into a fit of laughter. I know I shouldn't have, but couldn't help myself. Paul saw the funny side and laughed as well. We started talking about that night's game with AC Milan. I wasn't confident.

The thrashing in Barcelona had been followed by an Ipswich victory at Elland Road and these two defeats had dented confidence. At the time, we had no idea Ipswich would go into the final day of the season challenging for a place in the Champions

League themselves, and the final whistle brought a chorus of boos from all around Elland Road. Like most fans, I have criticised and cursed Leeds. On the odd occasion, I have even walked out before the end. But I have never been one to boo my own team and I wasn't going to start just because Ipswich had the audacity to beat us. I was worried about the Milan game though. The omens weren't good. One factor in our favour was that we had never lost at home to Italian opposition in Europe.

"First time for everything," was the retort of one cynical fan to this just prior to kick-off.

The rain which had been pouring incessantly all day just added to the less than cheerful mood which seemed to surround us as we made our way to Elland Road.

I bumped into Brighton John and asked how he had been after his fall from the train in Barcelona.

"Not good. It was hurting like mad when I got back. I saw the doctor and he said there was nothing seriously injured."

John then pulled his shirt up to reveal the whole side of his body was still black. The bruising was horrific, but he assured me it looked worse than it was. I certainly hoped so.

Walking up the steps to our seats in the Kop, we were met by the sight of the first eight rows at the South Stand being cordoned off. A quick glance at the East Stand showed four or five full rows covered in plastic sheeting. Watching the highlights on television later, I noticed the Kop was the same. What was all this about? A steward provided the answer.

"The advertising boards are so big for Champions League games that anyone sat at the front would not be able to see over them. UEFA stipulate the seats must remain empty."

I hadn't heard anything so stupid for a long time. Why couldn't all the boards be the same size as normal games? Due to these larger adverts, Elland Road's capacity was cut to just over 36,000 for every Champions League tie. That means 4,000 people are denied the chance to see Leeds every home game in Europe. Surely that can't be right? I would have thought UEFA would want more people watching football matches rather than less.

The first half against Milan finished goalless, but Leeds played well. The concourse underneath the Kop was buzzing with anticipation during the break.

"We can do this. AC Milan don't like it up 'em and Smithy is scaring them silly up front."

"They play in a boring league where you can pass the ball around for five minutes before a tackle comes in. They can't handle this. All we need is a goal and we're back in the competition."

We did well again after the break, but couldn't find a way through. I felt disappointed as the electronic scoreboard showed the 90 minutes were up, but at least we had our first point in the Champions League. Lee Bowyer had other ideas though.

Bow is a player that Leeds fans love. Arriving as a teenager in 1996, he didn't have the best of starts. His first season was a record-breaker for Leeds as we scored a pathetic 28 goals in 38 league games, the lowest number for any team avoiding relegation. Our strikeforce (if 'force' is the right word) of Ian Rush and Mark Hateley in a couple of early-season games had the combined age of 70. We were shit for most of that depressing season, but thankfully, Leeds and Bow had come a long way since those dark days.

Collecting the ball midway inside the Milan half and with time seemingly up, there appeared few options available. Bow looked up, obviously felt the same, and hit a speculative shot from 25 yards out.

The ball sailed towards keeper Dida who had time to adjust his feet before taking what should have been a routine catch next to his left-hand post. Whether he took his eye off the ball or let his mind wander as to who he would throw it to moments later, only the Brazilian keeper knows. But what happened next was as comical as it was decisive. In trying to catch the ball, Dida allowed it to slip from his grasp and it squirmed into the back of the net. *Thank You* may have been the name of the song by Dido which Eminem sampled for his huge hit *Stan*, but this was a case of "Thank you, Dida!"

It took a moment to sink in, but then it was pandemonium all around Elland Road. Bowyer ran towards the Kop closely followed by Smith and Matteo. The unthinkable had happened. We were ahead against the mighty Milan. Even the more sedate fans in the West Stand stood up and clapped!

The chant "Lee Bowyer, Lee Bowyer! Lee Bowyer!" boomed out with thousands of fingers pointing in unison towards our hero. It was a good enough feeling being stood in the Kop, but what can

Bowyer have felt like at that exact moment? I don't care how much money players earn, surely nothing can ever beat such a thrill? Chris Waddle once said that scoring a goal and celebrating with his team's supporters immediately afterwards was nearly as good as sex. All I can say is the Waddles' sex life must be something special.

Once everyone had calmed down, the game restarted but it was clear there was no way we were going to throw away our newfound advantage. The referee blew for full time and we celebrated again.

Besiktas' 3-0 win over Barcelona meant all four sides were level on three points in Group H with the Turkish club due at Elland Road in a week's time. Even the rain couldn't dampen our spirits as we filed out into the night. It was all such a contrast to six days earlier when the warm weather had been accompanied by a downcast mood. Now, the rain witnessed only happiness.

Leeds now faced the prospect of back-to-back games with Besiktas, including the emotional return to Istanbul, which would go a long way to deciding our fate. After the murder of two Leeds fans, Kevin Speight and Christopher Loftus, on the eve of the UEFA Cup semi-final with Galatasaray the previous season, this was a draw we could have done without. Only actually being paired with Galatasaray could have been worse and, understandably, Leeds facing a Turkish club again attracted headlines around the world.

The death of two Leeds fans had prompted the kind of emotional outpouring England had not seen since the death of Princess Diana three years earlier. I was booked on the club's one-day trip to Istanbul for that fateful game at the Ali Sami Yen Stadium, but after the events of the previous night, it was cancelled. I had followed the news as it broke on Sky until the early hours before finally grabbing a couple of hours sleep. I was not aware the trip was off until I arrived at Leeds-Bradford Airport and immediately drove to Elland Road where flags and shirts had already started to be left at both the main gates and the Billy Bremner statue in tribute. I didn't know either man, but they were Leeds fans and Leeds people. The whole city was plunged into mourning. It was an awful time.

I personally didn't want the semi-final to go ahead in Istanbul although I understand the reasons why it did. If we had backed out, the charitable souls at UEFA said they would kick us out of the competition. Murdering two innocent people must never be a passport to a final and Leeds, unfortunately, had to play.

I watched our 2-0 defeat in a Keighley pub later that night and, frankly, didn't give a damn whether we won, lost or drew. Football just didn't matter. It was the same at Aston Villa a few days later when we lost 1-0. I was sat on the back row of the away end, but I might as well have been sat on the hard shoulder of the nearby M6. I just did not feel part of it.

A lot of football fans, not just those supporting Leeds, felt the same. I was sat with Andy at Villa Park and after the game he travelled back to London by train.

He popped into a pub near Euston that was full of Chelsea and Newcastle fans following their FA Cup semi-final at Wembley earlier in the day. Andy had a Leeds badge attached to his coat which, under normal circumstances, would have resulted in some unwanted hassle. Or worse. He was just about to leave when one Chelsea fan came up to him with tears in his eyes saying how sorry he was.

"Those two lads could have been any one of us. We travel all over Europe watching Chelsea and we are so sorry over what happened."

Then he hugged Andy. It was a very emotional time for everyone and something I hope no other football club or city has to go through again. All those feelings came flooding back the moment the draw paired Leeds with another Istanbul club.

Both Leeds and Besiktas moved quickly after the draw to stress relations were good between the clubs and that 500 away fans would be allowed at each leg. As it happened, the Turkish club cancelled their planned supporters trip due to a lack of demand while Leeds took just 138 fans to the return leg.

A lot had been made in the national media about violence possibly occurring, but the day of the game passed off peacefully. It was also a day when I received one of my strangest pre-match phone calls. The voice on the other end of the line was Tanya Arnold, a reporter with the BBC.

"We are doing an outside broadcast from the car park behind the South Stand just before the game and wondered if you would be interviewed as a Leeds fan."

"Er, yeah. I'm up for it."

37

"Good. There will also be a Turkish journalist present and we want to do a feature on what you both think the atmosphere will be like and how the game will go."

It was settled. I had to meet Tanya and her crew at about quarter past six. I decided not to tell any of the lads because if I made a fool of myself, I'd prefer them not to see it. Plus, I didn't want any of them turning up to try and put me off. I was nervous enough already.

I arrived bang on time and before I knew it, I was perched on top of the BBC's outside broadcast van with Tanya, a cameraman and the Turkish journalist who, I have to say, was a rather attractive lass. It was time for my 15 minutes of fame.

As I climbed back down after the interview, I thought it had gone quite well. I hadn't stuttered over any answers and, even more surprisingly, had spoken some sense. My mobile phone soon started ringing with what I presumed would be congratulatory messages. No such luck.

"You pervert!", "What a lech!", and "I'm surprised you didn't dribble down the front of your jacket!" were three of the more choice comments I received from so-called mates. I didn't know what they were on about until I saw a video of the interview later on. When the Turkish journalist had been answering, I had spent the whole time staring at her, or more precisely ogling her, and at least twice, my eyes strayed up and down her body as I had a good, long look. I was horrified. I looked a right sex case. Needless to say, this has not been forgotten about since and is gleefully brought up by so-called 'mates'.

Towards the end of the interview, I had predicted a narrow 3-2 victory for Leeds even though we had stuttered again in the League the previous Saturday with a 1-1 draw at Derby. Besiktas had followed up their momentous win over Barcelona with a 5-1 thrashing of Ankara to go top of their domestic league.

My confidence had been restored by the win over Milan and Leeds followed that up tonight by producing one of the club's best performances in Europe. Before kick-off, the visiting players had handed bouquets of flowers to the United crowd in memory of the two Leeds fans who died in Istanbul. It was a welcome gesture and their generous nature extended to the pitch as they continued handing out gifts to Leeds.

Within 22 minutes, we were 3-0 in front thanks to goals from Lee Bowyer, Mark Viduka and Dominic Matteo. Lucas Radebe, who scores about as often as the Pope, even tried a shot but only succeeded in sending an effort that struck the corner flag. We were all in such high spirits that we just laughed. And so did Lucas.

Eirik Bakke made it 4-0 after half-time before Darren Huckerby and Bowyer rounded off an unbelievable night. News came through that Manchester United had lost 3-1 against PSV Eindhoven in Holland so we cheered again.

"Poor old Fergie! Good job one English side knows how to play in Europe!"

However, that was nothing compared to the roar that greeted the news that AC Milan had won in Barcelona. It took a few moments to sink in but then it dawned on us.

"We are top of the league, say we are top of the league!"

We were level on points with AC Milan, but due to having beaten them at Elland Road, we were, unbelievably, top of Group H! The scoreboard again flashed up the 6-0 scoreline just in case we had forgotten. No-one wanted to leave, but eventually we filed out into the cool night. The air was full of excited talk.

"A point in Istanbul and then a win at home to Barcelona and we're through."

"Sod a point. Let's beat them again and we'll be more or less through."

David O'Leary summed it up after the game when he told the press, "I'm starting to enjoy this Champions League lark!"

He wasn't the only one. The only cloud on the horizon was the return to Istanbul. But for the moment, we just wanted to savour the 'Joy of six'. So we did.

Chapter Four

The Return To Hell

"If you must leave your hotel over the next three days, you must tell me and I will ensure you are given an armed escort, no matter what the time of day or night. I am here to ensure your comfort and safety."

Welcome to Istanbul. Ercam was dressed in a sharp suit and joined by five similarly dressed men who greeted us the moment we stepped through passport control at Ataturk Airport. At first, I wondered who the hell they were. The guns resting on their hips were the first clue. Then Ercam stepped forward and said he was a senior policeman in Istanbul and explained that he and his colleagues would be based at our city centre hotel for the next three days. In the background were a line of uniformed officers, all armed, watching our every move. This was serious.

After the tragic events of the previous April when Christopher Loftus and Kevin Speight had been savagely murdered ahead of Leeds' UEFA Cup semi-final with Galatasaray, the police were taking no chances. The two stabbings had attracted headlines all around the world, with many asking serious questions over the lack of protection offered to the Leeds supporters by the local police in Taksim Square that fateful night. This time they had to be seen to do the right thing.

The previous season, I had been looking forward to visiting one of the most historic cities in the world and the place where it is said that Europe meets Asia. The murders put an end to that as the official one day trip was cancelled. Whitby John, Alec and the Doctor had all travelled independently so, on hearing the breaking news about the stabbings, my first thoughts were for them. Thankfully, they were fine.

I learned on a sombre train journey to Aston Villa a few days later that they hadn't seen any trouble throughout their stay. They had walked freely around Istanbul on the afternoon of the game when the media back home were telling us all Leeds fans had been confined to their hotels. The events in Taksim Square had been a horrible, tragic, isolated incident. Everyone's sympathies were with the families and friends of the two men. Their loved ones had travelled to Turkey to watch a football match and never returned. It was just too awful for words.

Galatasaray showed a disgraceful lack of respect in not wearing black armbands or having a minute's silence before the first leg that Leeds lost 2-0. It was left to the United fans to pay their own respects by turning away from the field and holding their arms up in the air while remaining silent. The Turks' response was to make sickening throat-cutting gestures at the visiting fans. Scum is too kind a word for them.

The return leg at Elland Road was a very emotional night. Thankfully, common sense had prevailed and UEFA, making a rare correct decision, ruled no away fans would be allowed to travel. The outrage that followed the events in Istanbul had seen Turkish restaurants and takeaways attacked in England. Having away fans at Elland Road would only inflame the situation.

Leeds took out £100,000 worth of advertisements in national newspapers on the morning of the return leg, appealing for calm. Emotions were running high in the city and a bus carrying the Turkish media had a window broken outside Elland Road an hour or so before kick-off. Many pubs in the city centre were full from lunchtime onwards and the atmosphere was as poisonous as I can recall. Two Leeds fans started fighting in the toilet of Spencer's with one accusing the other of trying to pickpocket him. It was that sort of day. The game finished 2-2 and Galatasaray were through, but I was just glad it was all over. I never wanted Leeds to draw a Turkish side ever again. Unfortunately, as football fans, we rarely get what we want.

The draw for the first group stage of the Champions League sees all 32 sides being split into four seeded groups. Leeds and Galatasaray were seeded in different groups so there was a possibility we would again face the Turkish club. "Please God, no," seemed to be the consensus of opinion in Leeds.

Thankfully we avoided them. Rangers, Sturm Graz and Monaco were instead handed the dubious pleasure of facing Galatasaray in Group D. I was glad. The relief was short-lived though and, moments later, it was clear we were going back. I didn't know much about Besiktas apart from that they were city rivals of Galatasaray.

Both Leeds and Besiktas acted swiftly. They were keen to foster good relations and both Leeds chairman, Peter Ridsdale, and Besiktas president, Serdar Bilgili, let everyone know via the media that they got on well. It was agreed 500 fans from either club should be allowed to travel, providing they were on official one day trips. It was hardly ideal because we would be escorted straight from the airport to the stadium without having a chance to explore Istanbul, but it was better than nothing. It was then that I received an offer I couldn't refuse.

"Would you like to travel on the two night press trip and cover the game?"

It took me about three seconds to decide. I'd love to.

My previous trips abroad covering football had been while reporting on Bradford City for the local paper, the *Telegraph & Argus*. I covered City for three enjoyable years from 1997, although being 'outed' as a Leeds fan by some unhappy Bantams on the internet was an experience and a half. Bradford folk don't like Leeds very much so, all of a sudden, I was about as popular as my namesake Peter (no relation!) had been during the Yorkshire Ripper trial.

Some wanted me banned from Valley Parade for life while away trips to Bury and Port Vale saw the travelling fans chanting "Richard Sutcliffe is a wanker!", much to the amusement of then manager Paul Jewell who said he agreed 100 per cent with them. Which was nice. Through my job I had covered a City friendly in Macedonia and a pre-season trip to St Kitts in the Caribbean. Both were very enjoyable, but following Leeds to Istanbul was a different prospect altogether. I couldn't believe my luck.

Fast forward a couple of weeks and here I was, part of the official press party, being met at passport control at Ataturk Airport.

It was here that Radio Leeds' Ian Dennis was the victim of a cracking wind-up from Leeds' Press Officer, Dick Wright.

West Yorkshire Police send their own officers to every Leeds away game to monitor the behaviour of travelling fans and offer help to the local force. Dick hatched his plan with their help. As we passed through passport control, Ian was pulled to one side by one of the police spotters. "Your name is on the list of people who

43

Interpol have told us should not be allowed into Turkey," growled the copper. "You are a hooligan."

The colour drained from Ian's face as he tried to protest. All he could think was Radio Leeds would have no coverage of the following night's vital game due to him having been deported.

"Th-th-there must be some mistake. I can't be on this list."

"There is no mistake, sir."

Ian was worried now, but at that exact moment he nervously glanced round and saw Dick doubled up in laughter. He had been well and truly had.

Once through passport control and with Ian suitably red-faced, Ercam, who we later discovered was the head of the Vice Squad in Istanbul, introduced himself. The welcoming speech raised a few eyebrows. If the police felt we needed an armed escort around the city, what sort of trip was this going to be?

We made our way out to the coach and Ercam gave the nod for the escort, which comprised both cars and motorbikes, to set off towards the Conrad International Hotel, our base for the next two days. The escort took us along the bank of the Bosphorus River and the locals gawped, obviously wondering who merited such a heavy police presence. Bill Clinton had visited Istanbul a few weeks earlier and we were told the security operation for tomorrow's match would be bigger than that afforded to the President of America.

Istanbul is where Europe ends and Asia starts, the Bosphorus marking the boundary of each. European Istanbul, which houses most of the tourist attractions, is further split by the Golden Horn with Old Istanbul to the south and Beyoglu in the north. Our hotel was based in the Beyoglu area, just a couple of minutes walk away from the Bosphorus with the Asian part of the city lying across the water. Besiktas' Inonu Stadium - described by no less than Pele as one of the most beautiful football grounds in the world - was about 20 minutes walk away along the river bank.

We drove past the stadium towards the hotel and it looked pleasant enough, nestled at the bottom of the hills leading away from the river and surrounded by trees. Several police cars were parked near the entrance of the hotel as we arrived. They really were taking no chances with safety this time.

Following Leeds in Europe is an expensive business so we try and cut costs at every turn. This has led to me staying in some hotels that would struggle to achieve one star status. The worst came before Leeds played Partizan Belgrade in the first round of the UEFA Cup. Due to the political situation in Kosovo, the first leg was moved from Yugoslavia to the neutral town of Herenveen in northern Holland. We opted to spend the night in Amsterdam (it is amazing how many Euro aways include a stop-off in the Dutch capital!) and Andy woke up the following morning covered in flea bites. The sign outside claiming the hotel was 'clean and simple' was obviously not to be taken literally, although at £10 a night we probably got what we paid for.

The hotel in Istanbul was in a different league to that with marble halls and chandeliers throughout. It was well out of my normal price range so I was determined to make the most of it. Leaving the room was a wrench although being charged £7 for a bottle of beer later that night took the shine off it slightly.

Under UEFA regulations, both clubs must hold a press conference on the eve of the game and David O'Leary was due to appear at 6pm ahead of his side training in the stadium. The main topic was whether young goalkeeper Paul Robinson would be up to the task of playing in such an important match due to first choice Nigel Martyn being out injured. O'Leary was adamant.

"Paul will one day take over from Nigel at this club and the next few weeks will see him growing into a man."

The press conference drew to a close and as the reporters filed their copy back to England, I took the chance to watch training for 20 minutes or so before deciding to walk back to the hotel. Big mistake. The *Yorkshire Post*'s Jeremy Cross joined me and it soon became obvious we were attracting some attention. It was dark and as we walked past a row of shops and cafes, I could feel all eyes looking towards these two pale, white faces. After leaving the stadium laughing and joking, we soon fell silent and remained that way for the 20 minute walk. I don't know whether the threat was real or imagined, but I was mightily glad to return to the hotel. I would be sticking to the coach or taxi at night for the rest of the trip. Indeed, the evening was spent at a fish restaurant located on a boat moored in the Golden Horn with taxis ferrying us all around. We had turned down the offer of a police escort.

The morning of the match dawned with bright sunlight shining over Istanbul. My usual routine when Leeds are in Europe is to pass the afternoon and early evening moving from bar to bar while savouring the atmosphere. I was working in Istanbul so this was hardly an option, and at £7 a bottle I don't think I could have afforded to anyway. Instead, I passed the morning playing tennis and then decided to head out for some sight-seeing after sneaking past the police in reception.

I wanted to visit the Grand Bazaar so caught a taxi to take me across the Golden Horn via Ataturk Bridge and into Old Istanbul. The Bazaar houses more than 4,000 shops as well as banks, workshops, mosques and police stations and is quite a sight. Almost anything can be bought here, legal or illegal, and if you only visit one place in Istanbul, this should be it. After returning to the hotel, I joined several of the journalists in walking the short distance to the shore of the Bosphorus where we enjoyed a leisurely meal.

My relaxed day was quite different from that being experienced by fans on the official day trip. Whitby John, Tally and the Doctor travelled with the club and were less than pleased to learn just a couple of days before departure that the whole trip would be alcohol-free. They would not, as they believed, be bussed to a bar well outside the city centre for the afternoon of the game. Instead, the police had decreed they would spend the two hours leading up to kick-off on a boat sailing down the Bosphorus. 500 places were available for the trip, but in the end only one plane was needed with 138 fans making the return to Istanbul.

Due to the murders of the previous April, Leeds' return to Turkey had attracted the attention of the world's media. When Whitby John arrived at Leeds-Bradford Airport, camera crews from Sky, BBC and ITV as well as a handful from abroad met him. The Doctor duly took centre stage as one live interview was taking place by poking his head in front of the camera and shouting, "Hello Scunthorpe!" No doubt this bemused the viewers at home watching the breakfast news. It probably also put them off their Corn Flakes.

The arrival of the Leeds fans in Turkey, many of whom had smuggled vodka and orange bottles onto the plane, threw the airport staff into a panic because they touched down at the same time as the Galatasaray squad returning from a Champions League tie with Rangers in Glasgow. Superb planning by someone. As a result, the Leeds fans were kept waiting on the tarmac until the Galatasaray squad were driving away from Ataturk Airport.

Eventually, the Leeds fans were allowed into the terminal to be met by hundreds of armed officers and enough camera flashbulbs to light up a small city. By this stage, most fans were now bored by the attention they were receiving, although Peter Ridsdale did turn up to thank them for travelling.

The previous April, Leeds fans had unfurled a 'Hello Hell, we are Leeds' banner on arrival, in response to the infamous welcome Galatasaray fans had given Manchester United and Chelsea in recent years. This time around, the Leeds fans contented themselves with a rather tuneless rendition of Rod Stewart's *Sailing* in anticipation of the forthcoming boat trip. The fans were escorted the short distance to the river where they were herded on to a ferry. A two hour cruise down the Bosphorus lay ahead. It was dark, so there wasn't even anything to look at from on deck.

"Ridsdale, Ridsdale give us a beer!" chanted the upper deck, but the Leeds chairman just waved back.

Fans and banners, including one with 'LUFSea' emblazoned across it, were draped over the side and the entire journey was broadcast live on Turkish Television, which must have made riveting viewing. A few Leeds fans then struck gold while sat below deck.

"Look at this lot. There are about ten bottles of wine down here that must be left over from a party. Let's get stuck in."

Quicker than you could say, "We haven't got a corkscrew", the bottles were open and being drunk. The captain of the ship came downstairs an hour later and was horrified to see all his wine had been swiped.

Eventually, the stadium floodlights came into view and the volume was cranked up.

"Glory, Glory Leeds United,
Glory, Glory Leeds United,
Glory, Glory Leeds United,
As the Whites go marching.
On and On! On and On! On and On! On and On!"

The home fans had been kept well away from the quay by a small army of policeman who sprang into action as the ferry docked. The ground was only a short distance away, but everyone from Leeds was forced on to four waiting buses with the police running alongside en route to the turnstiles.

"Why can't we walk? It's only about 200 yards."

47

"Either you get on the bus or you go home to England."

Hundreds of cameras followed the buses every move, but with so many reporters and police present, there was never going to be any potential flashpoint for trouble. The arrival of the Leeds fans had been timed to avoid the vast majority of the Besiktas supporters who seem to think taking their seat an hour before the game is cutting it fine. The media coach was not quite so fortunate.

We had left the hotel almost three hours before the scheduled 9.45pm kick-off for the short drive to the Inonu Stadium, and had only been travelling a couple of minutes when the first stone was thrown by a group of around 50 pumped-up Turks. The police, who were escorting us, moved them away from the coach in a bid to prevent any more missiles being thrown. That did not stop the home fans offering their own particular welcome.

"Leeds United, Fuck you! Fuck you!"

The coach moved on, but as we turned right into the approach to the stadium, there was an even larger mob of fans waiting and they were all singing the same song. A couple more missiles were thrown as we all moved away from the windows that thankfully remained intact. Once the coach had pulled up outside the press entrance, the police stood in two lines to ensure we didn't have any further problems. It wasn't much of an incident with only a couple of missiles thrown, but I was still relieved to finally be inside.

The game was still more than two hours away and yet half the stadium was already full. The noise was deafening. The tannoy boomed out some Turkish disco music, which was stopped at regular intervals to allow the home fans to shout out the names of their favourite players in unison. The hairs on the back of my neck were standing up already. It was a pleasant change from the Smashie and Nicey-style DJs who plague Premiership grounds. I hate these people with their banal comments and feeble attempts at generating an atmosphere. It is no wonder a large majority of fans in England refuse to take their seats until shortly before kick-off.

A banner reading 'England are shit' was unfurled behind the goal. It drew a "Can't argue with that" response from the press box, but bearing in mind our national side had lost at home to Germany and drawn with Finland inside the previous ten days, this was perhaps understandable. A 'Fuck off Leeds' banner also appeared on the opposite side of the stadium, but club officials swiftly confiscated it.

The first Leeds players appeared on the field about an hour before kick-off and the response was predictable as a wall of booing and jeering broke out. The home fans were trying hard to give their side the edge by psyching out the United squad. It clearly wasn't working though as the players met the abuse with prolonged icy stares.

Besiktas are undeniably the third club in Istanbul. Fenerbahce and Galatasaray are commonly accepted as the biggest two clubs in Turkey, and despite recent success, Besiktas are unlikely to change that. Football has enjoyed something of a boom period in Turkey in recent years after a long time in the doldrums. The 8-0 victory England enjoyed against Turkey as recently as 1987 is unlikely to ever be repeated again. Galatasaray also beat Arsenal in the UEFA Cup final while the national side reached the quarter-finals of Euro 2000 before bowing out against Portugal.

Once inside, I couldn't quite understand Pele's claim that it was one of the most beautiful football grounds in the world. True, the setting is very pleasant due to the stadium being nestled at the foot of hills leading up from the Bosphorus. Trees also surround the stadium on all four sides. And compared to Galatasaray's Ali Sami Yen Stadium, which we drove past on the way home and is boxed in between tower blocks and a motorway flyover, Inonu is positively regal. But surely there are countless other stadiums in the world which are nicer than this? I bet there's even a few in Turkey.

Leeds' 6-0 triumph three weeks earlier had clearly wounded Besiktas and left them desperate for revenge. The crowd were getting more and more worked up and the arrival of the small band of away fans was met by more booing. The chanting was incessant.

"Leeds United. Fuck you! Fuck you!"

The Leeds fans battled valiantly to make their voices heard, but their efforts were drowned out. The press box is to the left of where the away fans were sat, flanked by hundreds of policeman, but all I could hear were the fanatical home fans. The Leeds players looked on impassively though and were clearly in the mood to silence the locals.

After what had gone before, the kick-off was almost an anti-climax. Eirik Bakke fired Leeds best effort straight at the keeper in the sixth minute, but that was about it in terms of excitement. Since watching my first Leeds game - a 3-3 draw at home to West

Ham in November, 1981 - I have seen some superb games and I have also seen some shockers. Goalless draws at home to Reading in August 1987 and Derby in January 1997 were particularly dreadful and probably my two least enjoyable games. The latter came in George Graham's first season when the *Yorkshire Evening Post* wired up a United fan to see when he became the most excited. True to form, the game finished goalless and the fan's heartbeat rose to its highest level while eating a pie at half-time.

The second half in Istanbul ranked alongside those goalless draws with Reading and Derby in terms of entertainment, but the most important factor was we had gained a vital Champions League point. Even better, we were still top of the group after four games.

The only interesting aspect of the second half had been a huge fight breaking out on the opposite side of the pitch when two rival gangs of home fans, obviously frustrated by the dull football, clashed. The police soon charged in.

"If they are not careful, some of those Turks will end up hurting themselves," remarked one Leeds fan before adding with perfect comic timing, "With a bit of luck."

The Leeds fans were held in the stadium after the final whistle before being bussed to the airport and their flight back to Yorkshire. There had been no trouble involving the English and the world's camera crews looked almost disappointed.

To get to the post-match press conference, I had to make my way to the other side of the stadium. I was shown the way by a Besiktas official and as we walked round, a Turkish lad was swapping his scarf with one of the Leeds fans. The official was delighted.

"Did you see that? That is the spirit that exists between the two clubs. That is what football is all about."

I agreed that was what the game should be about, but pointed out what had happened to the media coach en route to the stadium.

"No, that must have been Galatasaray fans. Our fans are not like that."

"Well most of them had black and white shirts on so I doubt they supported Galatasaray."

He wasn't having it, but as I was more interested in getting to the press conference rather than arguing with this gentleman, I walked off. It proved to be the right decision because the press conference was a classic.

David O'Leary walked in, and straight away the mood of the Turkish journalists was apparent. They had expected their side to avenge the 6-0 drubbing suffered in Yorkshire, but Leeds had frustrated the home side. I couldn't help but laugh at the first question.

"Why did you come to Turkey? Was it to fight or to play a football game?"

O'Leary looked genuinely puzzled, but eventually replied, "I am not going to answer that."

It then got even more bizarre.

"From the first minute of the game, you made your substitutes warm up in front of the Besiktas coaches. Was that done on purpose to decrease the concentration of Besiktas coach, Nevio Scala?"

O'Leary had had enough. "UEFA stipulate where the subs should warm up, not me. I have answered your questions politely, but if you won't ask me any proper football questions, I will move on to my good friends in the English press."

Despite the ludicrous start to the press conference, the pride felt by the Leeds boss shone through as he discussed the game.

"We came here without a goalkeeper and missing midfielders, defenders and our top scorer so this is a great point. The quality of our football was not good enough, but we tried to do our best. It has been a difficult journey for our fans and I was fearful when I arrived in the city. But I have to say the Turkish people have behaved very well and I thank them."

Returning to Istanbul was always going to be an emotional experience for fans and players alike. The team had passed yet another important test with flying colours and were now in with a real chance of qualifying for the second group stage of the Champions League against all the odds. All that stood between us and a place in the next stage were games with Barcelona and AC Milan. Simple!

Chapter Five

The Italian Job

In many ways, the 1980s were a miserable time for Leeds United. The Revie era was just a fading memory while the club's revival under Howard Wilkinson did not truly gather pace until promotion was won in May, 1990.

Growing up watching the likes of Ronnie Robinson, John Stiles and Ken De Mange bumble their way around the old Second Division left me wondering if I would ever see Leeds take on the likes of Manchester United and Liverpool never mind Barcelona and AC Milan. Stoke once thrashed us 6-2 at the old Victoria Ground and goalkeeper Mervyn Day responded ahead of the following season's fixture by pledging there was no way he would be beaten six times again. He was right. Stoke won 7-2.

A couple of years later, we suffered the insult of our captain Mark Aizlewood celebrating a winning goal at home to Walsall by running towards the Kop and flicking two 'V' signs at us. Needless to say, it was not a Winston Churchill-style victory salute and he never played for Leeds again.

There were one or two glimmers of hope during our eight year stay in the Second Division. We reached the semi-final of the FA Cup and the play-off final in 1987 under Billy Bremner only to lose both games. There was also John Sheridan. Shez was, and will probably always remain, my favourite Leeds player. Frustratingly inconsistent at times, he was the only Leeds player in a very average side capable of producing a touch of genius. On some afternoons, he seemed like the only man capable of passing the ball to a team-mate.

My favourite memory of Shez came at Bramall Lane. Leeds were not having the best of days and Ken De Mange was looking particularly lost in midfield. Shez, seeming to share the frustrations of everyone stood in the away end as De Mange hesitated while in possession, simply ran up and barged his own team-mate off the ball before launching a Leeds attack.

Shez apart, however, the 1980s were not a great time for a club who just a decade or so earlier had been one of the best in Europe. We always seemed to be on the verge of one crisis or another. If it wasn't having to sell the ground to the council to stave off the threat of bankruptcy, it was having the terraces closed by the FA after Newcastle's Kevin Keegan was hit by a missile thrown from the crowd.

Fast forward to the year 2000 and a home win over Barcelona would be enough to see us go through at their expense. It all seemed slightly unreal. When we lost 4-0 in the Nou Camp, the odds on us being in this position would have been as long as those on Sir Alex Ferguson being offered the freedom of Leeds. And even if we failed to beat Barcelona, we still had a second chance with the visit to AC Milan a fortnight later.

The histories of the three clubs over the past 20 years could not be more contrasting. While we were crashing to regular defeats against the likes of Shrewsbury, Hull and Plymouth, Barcelona finished as runners-up in the European Cup under Terry Venables. Milan, meanwhile, won consecutive European Cups in 1989 and 1990.

I met Tally in The Britannia pub in Holbeck about an hour before kick-off and, as usual, it was packed. Holbeck is a fairly typical working class district of Leeds, a million miles away from the Harvey Nichols image that the city centre enjoys. Holbeck has row upon row of red brick terraced houses, with a large green the focal point of the area. The Britannia is situated at the edge of this green and flanked on either side by shops.

My favourite pre-match pub tends to change every couple of years. I have never liked The Old Peacock situated directly behind the South Stand on the opposite side of Elland Road. Drinking lager out of plastic glasses while listening to away fans chanting is hardly my idea of a good time. Instead, I have switched between several pubs within walking distance of Elland Road including The White Hart, The Wheatsheaf, The Waggon & Horses and now The Britannia.

The White Hart lies about ten minutes walk away from Elland Road up the hill in Beeston. It was here that I treated Paul, a

Manchester United supporting mate, to the unique atmosphere of a Leeds pub before a game with our deadliest rivals. This was before the police stipulated that all Leeds-Manchester United games must kick off at 12 noon. Sky was covering the match live so it was switched to 4pm on a Sunday. The White Hart was rammed from midday, and in the two hours leading up to kick-off I think every Leeds song was given an airing.

After his experience the previous year when the away fans had been ambushed leaving Elland Road, Paul wanted to sit in the home section with me so he could get away without any hassle. The strict understanding was he would keep his mouth shut if they scored. Not that he had any intention of cheering for his team, knowing what the response of those around him would be.

Paul therefore joined us in The White Hart and watched open-mouthed as we worked ourselves into a frenzy as kick-off approached. At one stage, the whole pub seemed to be jumping up and down in unison. We were both sat in the South Stand that afternoon as Leeds won 2-1 and Paul had a close escape during the half-time break when he bumped into an old schoolmate from Keighley in the toilets.

"Hiya, Paul. What are you doing here? Shouldn't you be sat in the South East corner with the other away fans?"

The toilets suddenly fell silent and Paul could feel everyone staring at him. Moments later, he came rushing out of the toilet looking like he had seen a ghost and muttering, "I'm off back to my seat."

He only told me what had happened later that night.

The mood in The Britannia ahead of the Barcelona game was one of quiet confidence although few seemed to believe we would be in the second group stage by the end of the night.

We needed a good start and it duly arrived in the now familiar guise of Lee Bowyer. Leeds won a free-kick just a few yards in from the left flank. "Whip it in quickly!" was the advice from those around me in the Kop. Whether that is what Bow intended to do or not only he knows, but he curled in a deep cross which, from the opposite end, seemed to be inviting a Leeds team-mate to throw himself at the ball. At the last moment, however, the ball failed to dip and with the Barcelona keeper now out of position it sailed over his head before landing in the back of the net.

Elland Road erupted!

I was halfway through a burger, which I duly launched into the air in celebration before Drew dived on my back. If it landed on anyone, I'm sorry!

"You fucking beauty, Bow! What a start!"

The players on the pitch matched the joyful reaction in the stands as Olivier Dacourt and Ian Harte mobbed Bowyer as he ran to the crowd. The fans of Leeds were united in voice.

"We're all going on a European tour, AGAIN!

A European Tour, AGAIN!

A European Tour, AGAIN!"

Alan Smith went close a couple of minutes later, but Barcelona gradually took control and play soon resembled a game of attack and defence. Thankfully, Paul Robinson was having the game of his life. The rookie keeper stopped everything the might of Barcelona could throw at him with an amazing display. Every minute seemed to be taking forever and I seriously wondered if my watch had stopped. I bit my nails and prayed for the end. Leeds were having trouble even getting out of their own half so this really was a back-to-the-walls effort. Every tackle was greeted with a huge cheer but still the seconds ticked away slowly.

Barcelona got the ball in the net after 75 minutes when Alfonso's shot wriggled through only for Rivaldo to be ruled offside. We breathed a huge sigh of relief. It felt like three hours had elapsed when the clock on the electronic scoreboard finally reached 90 minutes. All eyes were on the touchline as the fourth official raised the board to indicate how many minutes stoppage time would be played.

"Four minutes?! Bloody hell, he must be on Fergie time."

"Where the fuck has he got that amount of time from?"

The groans all around Elland Road told their own story. We had another four minutes of this torture ahead of us.

"I paid £22 for this ticket to put myself through this agony. I haven't been so nervous since I lost my cherry," was how one lad put it.

We tried to lift the players again with one last roar. All eyes were now on the referee as we pleaded for the final whistle. The four minutes of stoppage time had elapsed when Barcelona launched one last attack and Philip Cocu sent the ball forward in desperation.

"Blow your fucking whistle, ref!"

Substitute Gerard met the cross with a fine header only for the ball to crash against the post. 36,000 hearts then skipped a beat as it rebounded into the path of Rivaldo.

"No! Anyone but him."

The Brazilian hit the ball cleanly first time past the despairing dive of Robinson and the scores were level. The visitors' bench jumped to their feet as the Barcelona players and staff mobbed the man who had kept them in the Champions League. I was stunned into silence. I wasn't alone either. This was a much worse feeling than that which had followed 1860 Munich's stoppage time goal earlier in the season. We had been through every emotion in the 94 minutes and now I simply felt dreadful.

The final whistle went moments later and I couldn't speak. Everyone around me was screaming "Cheat!" at the referee, but I was unable to join in. I wanted to but I couldn't. We had been so close. The players were just as frustrated. Alan Smith squared up to Barcelona skipper Sergi and had to be pulled away by Gary Kelly.

On the balance of play, we had been lucky to get a point but rational thinking is not the order of the day when your team has just been denied a famous victory by a very, very late goal.

"It's a conspiracy. UEFA want teams like Barcelona through and not us. I bet the referee was under orders to play until they scored."

We had one last chance but the San Siro is hardly the sort of place you want to visit needing a point. I had no doubt Barcelona would thrash Besiktas so we could not afford to lose.

The moment the draw had been made back in August, it was clear Milan was set for a mass invasion from Leeds. The format of the Champions League means fans can plan a trip up to two or three months in advance rather than at short notice as is the case with the UEFA Cup. Therefore, with time to save up for the visit to Milan it meant 7,000 fans travelled from England to cheer United on.

The sheer volume of people descending on Milan caused air prices to rocket so, yet again, it was up to Whitby John to find us an alternative route. Eventually, he settled on Verona, about 100 miles east of Milan with a double-decker coach hired to transport all 57 of us to our hotel.

We arrived at Stansted on a cold Tuesday morning in an excited mood. The usual suspects were all present with Alec, the Doctor,

Whitby John, Keith, Tally and Vodka Pete all enjoying a couple of quick liveners in the airport bar ahead of the flight.

Pete had earned his nickname in Moscow the previous season while attempting to drink the Russian capital's entire stock of their national drink during our three day stay. Vodka Pete was also hoping to meet his son Vinnie, who is stationed in Germany with the Army, on this trip to Milan.

I was eagerly looking forward to the trip because Milan has a reputation as being one of the most glamorous cities in the world. It is also accepted as the fashion capital of Europe.

A medical conference was being held in Milan throughout our stay and this caused a few problems in finding a hotel. The fact there were 57 of us didn't help either. After the fiasco of Barcelona where we spent hours looking for a hotel, we vowed never to travel without accommodation again and Whitby John duly found us a motel about ten miles outside the centre of Milan. We arrived shortly after midday and after dropping off our bags, a quick walk round the area suggested we would be much better off in the city centre. It looked as dull as you could imagine with just a couple of bars and shops. It also didn't look like the sort of place that would be open late the following night should we want to celebrate qualifying for the next stage.

We arrived at Stazione Centrale as the afternoon was drawing to a close in Milan. Office workers were starting to make their way home, stopping only to glance at the seven Englishmen looking like what we were, lost tourists. I tried to stop a couple of Italians to ask which route we should take to reach the main city centre area, but they shied away with genuine fear in their eyes. The arrival of thousands of English football fans had obviously made the locals apprehensive. We wouldn't know just how nervous until the following day.

We enjoyed a pleasant night in the centre of Milan with a highlight being a chance meeting with a lad who plays the character Richie in the soap, *Emmerdale*. An EastEnders man myself, I didn't recognise him but some of the others did so we chatted for a while. He was enjoying a break from filming and had decided to travel to Italy to cheer on his favourite team with some of his mates. Top man!

We took the obligatory photo with Tally deciding to mark it by dropping his trousers at the camera. We told our new friend, Richie, that we would be selling a story about him trying to shag Tally to *The Sunday Sport* the following weekend and he just replied, "So long as I get half the money, lads!"

We started to drift away from the centre as the bars began closing because we were hoping to find a lively nightclub. We eventually got chatting to a local who worked in a bar and he pointed us in the right direction. This is something we do all the time and it usually pays off. It did again in Milan because he told us about a strip club where we enjoyed a cracking couple of hours. Billy and Mark, a couple of Leeds fans we had met earlier in the evening, were also in there, with Mark being dragged up on stage by one of the dancers. He was then stripped and locked in a cage at the side of the stage, much to our amusement.

Unfortunately, a group of Leeds fans were not so lucky in Milan when they asked a local for directions to a lively club. After stepping out of a couple of taxis, they were immediately attacked in what had all the hallmarks of a pre-arranged ambush. The local thugs who were also shouting "Remember Istanbul!" stabbed one Leeds fan. Thankfully, he made a full recovery from his injuries. News of the stabbing spread quickly on the morning of the game as friends and family back home checked, via mobiles, that loved ones were okay.

We had wandered around the city centre the previous evening and, frankly, I was disappointed. It was no more impressive in daylight. I had been expecting a much more glamorous and vibrant city than the one we found. Milan Cathedral is the focal point with its marble facade shaped into pillars, statues and ornamental turrets. It also seems to tower over its surroundings and can therefore be used as a point of reference when finding your way round. The Cathedral looks out onto a huge square, which is a pleasant place to pass a few minutes.

A wedding party were having their photographs taken and this brought back memories of Alec in Moscow the previous season. Despite the temperatures dipping well below freezing, it seems a tradition for Russian newlyweds to have their photos taken in Red Square. Alec saw this and decided to get in on the action. In a 20 minute spell, he moved between the wedding parties and kissed around 15 brides. The thought of these couples looking back at their wedding photo albums in 20 years time with Alec's face beaming back always makes me smile.

The area around the Cathedral is pleasant, but walk just a couple of minutes down the road and the city has an altogether grubbier feel. Milan looked like what it is, an industrial northern town, and certainly not what I'd been expecting.

I also wasn't impressed with the local police force's decision to make Milan an alcohol-free zone on match day. With the arrival of 7,000 Leeds fans making the local police paranoid, all the bars had been told to either close or sell just soft drinks.

We were later told the media had spent the past few days running scare stories about the forthcoming invasion from 'an army of English hooligans'. The poor reputation of the English football fan goes before us across Europe. When we were drawn to face Partizan Belgrade in the UEFA Cup in 1999, the Yugoslav media proudly announced 'Tony Blair to send 500 hooligans to Belgrade'. The thought of the Prime Minister dipping into Government funds to send Leeds fans to a Euro away was so ridiculous it was laughable.

Despite the alcohol ban in MIlan, we were confident of finding a way round it. Our first port-of-call was a Scottish pub situated just behind the Cathedral.

"We are serving alcohol, but if anyone wants a drink then they must buy a sandwich as well."

This meant a pint and a sandwich cost around £7 so we had just one and left. The bars had been open near our hotel, but with that area being as dull as Grimsby on a wet Monday morning, we opted to persevere with the city centre.

Five bars later and with not one "Si!" meeting our pleas for a drink, we at last found a pavement cafe willing to serve us so we stayed for a couple of hours. The pattern of being turned away from several cafes before finally finding a welcoming bar continued throughout the afternoon. Some Leeds fans had given up after their first couple of refusals, but the veterans of previous trips found their way round the ban.

"That's the difference between us and the fans who have discovered football since Euro 96, we know we'll always get a drink somehow."

Miles, a mate from Tadcaster, was grateful for the help of a friendly bar owner who wanted, understandably, to earn himself a few lira. Miles had befriended him the previous night so when they returned midway through the afternoon of the match, the owner welcomed them with open arms.

"You boys sit down there and I will bring some dirty plates from the kitchen to put on the table in front of you. If the police come here, you must say you have just finished your meal. I can only sell alcohol to people eating food."

This left everyone happy and when the police came in to look round later that afternoon, Miles started stroking his stomach while saying, "What a marvellous meal."

The police, pleased the law was being obeyed, left. They returned an hour or so later to see the same plates sat on the table in front of the same faces, but didn't seem to work out what was going on.

We continued to find the odd bar owner willing to serve us although many stuck to the ban.

"I want to serve you, but I cannot because of the police. The police do not want you to have a drink."

"Stop us having a drink before a game? There's more chance of finding an Italian tank from World War II that went forwards instead of backwards."

We rounded off the afternoon by visiting a Chinese restaurant, passing a couple of enjoyable hours with a meal and a few more drinks. Despite the inconvenience of the alcohol ban, it had been a good afternoon but as kick-off approached I started to suffer from PMT (Pre-Match Tension). I had really enjoyed the Champions League and I was desperate for our run to continue. But if that was to happen, we had to take at least a point off AC Milan in the imposing San Siro.

Like Barcelona, AC Milan are a club that typifies what the Champions League is all about. They boast a proud history with five European Cups to their name, possess numerous glamorous players, and have one of the best stadiums in Europe.

The Stadio Giuseppe Meazza, or San Siro as it more commonly known, was built in 1926 and has undergone three major developments since. The most recent came ahead of the 1990 World Cup when a third tier was added. The San Siro, which was renamed after popular Italian striker Giuseppe Meazza following his death in 1979, is an awesome sight whether viewed from inside or outside the stadium. With no running track and the advertising hoardings being close to the pitch, the San Siro also has an intimacy few major stadiums can match. Shared by both AC and Inter Milan since the end of World War II, the only downside is the shocking state of the playing surface. The steep stands, weekly use and damp Milanese weather have all combined to create a poor pitch that must be re-laid at regular intervals. It was certainly not at its best the night Leeds took on Milan with the ball bobbling about all over the place.

AC Milan had met Leeds just once before this season when the *rossoneri* triumphed 1-0 in the 1973 Cup Winners' Cup final. The game was dogged by controversy though with the referee being subsequently banned from officiating ever again by UEFA after a display that infuriated United. Leeds would go on to reach the European Cup final two years later, but for Milan it was, by their high standards, the start of a bleak period as they failed to win another European trophy for 16 years.

We arrived at the San Siro shortly after kick-off by tram. Keith was obviously a bit over-excited as he jumped off the tram and shouted, "English bastidos, cappiche?" He followed this with "Come on!"

To this day, we don't know who he was offering out because as we were the only people around.

It didn't take us long to locate the away fans turnstiles with what seemed like a mass army of policemen suspiciously eyeing the visiting Englishmen entering the stadium. A small group of Leeds fans had been attacked outside the stadium due to one of them wearing a shirt of Milan's deadly rivals, Juventus, but we made our way in with no problems.

Our tickets were for the bottom tier of the North Stand, which provides a tremendous view of the pitch. As is the case with Dutch stadia, the front row of the stands behind the goal at the San Siro are situated higher than the crossbar which means even those fans at the front have a good view.

The first few minutes were played to the backdrop of flares being waved by the home fans and vociferous support from the 7,000 Leeds fans. There aren't many clubs who can muster such a large support for a non-final tie played abroad and it made me proud as I looked around the San Siro. It must have also helped the players because we started well.

Unfortunately, disaster struck midway into the first half when Gary Kelly was adjudged to have handled and the referee pointed to the spot. The offence had been straight in front of us and was a clear case of the ball striking Kelly's arm before he could pull it away, but the protests did no good. A fight had broken out between two Leeds fans to our right moments earlier, but the penalty put an end to that as everyone prayed Paul Robinson could pull off a vital save.

Standing directly behind the goal as Andriy Shevchenko stepped forward, I, in common with thousands of others, waved my arms frantically to try to put the Ukrainian off. He struck the spot-kick well to Robinson's left, but the Leeds keeper dived the wrong way. At last, however, we enjoyed a bit of luck as the ball struck the outside of the post and bounced to safety. Cue celebrations of joy tinged with relief behind Robinson's goal.

"Come on Leeds, don't waste this now!"

The moment we had been longing for came on the stroke of half-time when Lee Bowyer curled a corner towards the near post and Dominic Matteo, who had nudged ahead of his marker, flicked the ball past Dida and into the net.

It was one of those few moments when I lost myself in a football stadium. Gordon Strachan's strike against Leicester in our promotion year to clinch a vital 2-1 win, David Seaman's penalty save against Spain in Euro 96 and Brian Gayle's own goal against Sheffield United which clinched the League title for us in 1992 are three of my all-time favourite football moments. The celebrations that met Matteo's goal were just as euphoric.

Whitby John jumped on my back while I vaguely recall Tally screaming into my face, but apart from that I can't remember anything else. I was later told I ended up on the floor while screaming "What a goal!" Quite strange behaviour when you look at it in a rational manner, but what place does rationality have at a vital football match between Leeds and AC Milan?

Leeds had a priceless goal and the celebrations continued throughout the 15 minute half-time break. We had one foot in the next phase.

The traditional bare-chested, shirt-waving rendition of "Champions of Europe!" was performed with as mush passion as I can ever recall. Waving a coat and shirt above your head for 15 minutes while singing along is tiring so I was shattered by the time the players came back out after the break. I soon found the energy to get behind the lads though.

Leeds were attacking our end in the second half, but in truth, we didn't see too much of the ball. Instead, Milan did most of the attacking and Serginho equalised with about 20 minutes left. Now I was tense. That emotion was obviously shared by everyone around me as nervous looks were exchanged. We were so close from either success or failure.

Thankfully, Milan seemed to ease off and the game meandered towards the final whistle. After the heartbreak of Rivaldo's last-gasp goal at Elland Road a fortnight earlier, I couldn't relax until referee Kim Nielsen (the one who sent David Beckham off in France '98, top man!) finally signalled it was all over.

After all the tension of the previous 90 minutes, my initial feeling was one of anti-climax but that soon gave way to pure, undiluted joy as the celebrations began. We had clinched second place in Group H. Barcelona had thrashed Besiktas 5-0 but no-one cared. They were now in the UEFA Cup while we were still in the Champions League! As the Milanese drifted away, the Italian police treated us to the now customary 90 minute detention inside the stadium. Not that we were too bothered as the party continued in the lower tier of the North Stand.

Eddie Gray and Paul Robinson were the first to emerge from the dressing room area and back onto the pitch. The rest of the squad, all wearing Leeds United tracksuits, soon followed. The response was swift.

"Leeds team, give us a song,
Leeds team, Leeds team, give us a song!"

Gary Kelly was the first to step forward and as he beckoned us to be quiet, an eerie hush descended on the San Siro.

"Let's go fucking mental! Let's go fucking mental! Na na na na, Leeds! Na na na na, Leeds!"

As Kelly bounced up and down on the pitch, he was soon joined by all his team-mates and 7,000 backing singers. It was a wonderful moment I will never forget. Just a day earlier,

Manchester United captain Roy Keane had dismissed a section of the Old Trafford support as 'the prawn sandwich brigade'. These fans, admittedly many of them sat in the corporate seats, were too quick to criticise and knew nothing about football, claimed Keane. Well, he should have been in the San Siro that night to see what real fans are like. In the current football world where many Premiership players earn more in a week than the vast majority of fans take home in a year, a gulf has opened up. Relating to someone earning £30,000 plus per week is not easy. But in Milan, I felt part of a very special moment.

Gary Kelly was obviously enjoying himself as he stepped forward once more to call for quiet. He then placed his shirt on the ground, sat on it and shouted, "Sit down, if you hate Man U!"

We didn't need asking twice. Kelly was soon drowned out as everyone retook their seats while singing about our hated rivals. Alan Smith joined the party with a rendition of "We're Leeds and we're proud of it!" so we sang along again.

Calm returned and Lee Bowyer took centre stage before trying to start another song. We were left scratching our heads. We couldn't understand a word. The response took just a couple of seconds.

"What the fucking hell was that?!"

A suitably shame-faced Bowyer then ran to the far end of the stadium with the verdict of "Time to go . . . " ringing in his ears from both his team-mates and the fans. David O'Leary and Peter Ridsdale emerged to join the party with the Leeds chairman the next to call for quiet.

"I bet he starts singing *Money, Money, Money* now we're in the next stage," Whitby John shouted, which made us all laugh.

Ridsdale managed only "Marching on . . . " before being drowned out. I couldn't imagine Ken Bates leading the Chelsea masses in such a way, nor Martin Edwards at Manchester United for that matter. Ridsdale demonstrated that he is a fan at heart. He was as happy as we were. It was a memorable end to a wonderful evening in Leeds United's history.

As the players left the field, I suddenly felt very, very tired. It had been a long day and a night where Leeds had tested my nerves to the full. Whitby John had booked a coach to take us back to our hotel and we all had a slip of paper telling us where it would be parked in the streets outside the San Siro. The buses used to ferry the official supporters trips around were all parked together just outside the away enclosure while ours was some distance away. We tried to walk through the massed ranks of police, but they just shoved us back and pointed towards the official buses. We tried to explain, but it soon became clear we were wasting our time. Eventually, we sneaked through a hole in a fence and found the coach with no problem. By midnight, we were on the way back to our hotel while the official coaches were held for another hour or so.

Such a famous night should have led to a wild night of celebration, but all I wanted to do was go to bed. I felt drained and within about five minutes of arriving at the hotel, I was asleep. Most others felt the same, although Alec and Keith ventured back into Milan only to return a couple of hours later complaining that everywhere was shut.

We had to travel the 100 miles back to Verona early the following morning and most of us agreed it had been a fantastic night, but that Milan had been a disappointment.

"Milan is a dump, but I suppose I'll have to come back when we reach the final in May," was how one of the lads summed it up. Now we were getting carried away!

The trip home was uneventful, although I did bump into former Great Britain rugby league international, Karl Harrison, at Verona Airport. I support Keighley Cougars, and with Karl being coach of the club, I wandered over for a chat. Karl is a huge fan of Leeds and once changed the kick-off for Keighley versus Sheffield to 1pm so he could watch Leeds at Bradford City later the same afternoon. He was as elated as the rest of us following the draw in Milan and already thinking of our next opponents.

"Wouldn't it be great to get someone like Real Madrid or Bayern Munich in the next round. We probably won't go through, but it would be wonderful to watch us in the Bernabeu. I'll have to make sure I change training that week and give the lads a couple of days off!"

Quite a few Leeds fans had decided to travel via Verona and despite being shattered due to the early morning start, there was no way the grins would be disappearing from our faces for quite some time.

Few had given us a chance in such a tough group and yet we came within 20 minutes of finishing top. We took four points off

Milan, four off Besiktas and also managed to knock out one of the biggest clubs in the world. All this was achieved without the likes of David Batty, Harry Kewell, Stephen McPhail and Michael Bridges for long periods. Not bad for a team dismissed as "poor" by Barcelona's Frank de Boer after our defeat in the Nou Camp. Hope you enjoyed the UEFA Cup, Frank!

Chapter Six

Mission Impossible II

Imagine the reaction today if Norwich City suddenly announced they were adopting the red and blue of Barcelona as their new team colours in a bid to emulate the Catalan giants. The laughter would reverberate from here to Spain. The words 'ideas', 'above' and 'station' would no doubt figure in most responses.

But in 1961, new Leeds manager Don Revie did something very similar. Leeds were then just a struggling Second Division club, more than £100,000 in debt, and flirting with relegation. Revie, keen to change the downcast mood surrounding the club, decided to ditch United's traditional yellow and blue colours in favour of the all white of Real Madrid – the club he wanted Leeds to emulate.

Real's five successive European Cup triumphs from 1956 meant they were the club everyone aspired to be. For Revie to aim so high seemed ludicrous. But the great man did just what he promised. Promotion in 1964 was followed by a wonderful decade as Leeds won two League titles, two Inter-Cities Fairs Cups, an FA Cup and a League Cup. Cruelly, Leeds were denied the number of honours their dominance deserved as they finished as runners-up an amazing five times in the League. They were also beaten finalists twice in the FA Cup and once in the Cup Winners' Cup.

Revie left to manage England in the summer of 1974 and the team he had built went on to reach the European Cup final the following year only to lose to Bayern Munich.

Revie would have loved to have seen his Leeds side take on the great Real Madrid in European competition for the first time, but it was not to be. Instead, that honour went to the man we all hope will bring those glory days back to Elland Road, David O'Leary.

The Irish defender initially joined Leeds as a player in the summer of 1993. A Highbury legend after making a club record 558 League appearances for Arsenal, O'Leary's career in West

Yorkshire was short-lived. He played just ten games before retiring due to injury and we all presumed that would be the last we'd see of him. But George Graham's arrival at Elland Road as manager in September, 1996, brought O'Leary back to Yorkshire as the club's new assistant boss. The pair started the long process of turning Leeds' fortunes around. When Graham quit to manage Spurs two years later, his assistant was also expected to return to North London.

Leeds had initially wanted Martin O'Neill to replace Graham, but Leicester refused us permission to speak to their manager. As fans we made it clear who we wanted, with O'Leary's name being sung long and loud during matches at home to Leicester (ironically) and then in the UEFA Cup against Roma. O'Leary was duly appointed, gave the all-conquering youth side their chance and the progress since then has been startling.

The point gained in Milan had brought about a general shift in the mood around Leeds. Knocking out Barcelona and taking four points off AC Milan meant the inferiority complex of the first group phase had given way to a much more confident air. We were worthy after all.

Despite this new-found confidence, the draw for the second group phase still brought a sharp intake of breath around the city. I had been hoping we'd draw another of Europe's biggest clubs, but I wasn't expecting it to be quite as tough. We were in Group D with the Champions League holders Real Madrid, Serie A champions Lazio, and Belgian champions Anderlecht.

The format of the Champions League sees two of the second phase group games take place in November and December before the competition enjoys a ten week break. It then resumes in mid-February with the final four matches taking place inside just five weeks. This means the opening two games set the tone for the whole group with a couple of early defeats making qualification almost impossible. Unfortunately for Leeds, the visit of Real Madrid to Elland Road being followed by a trip to Rome and a meeting with Lazio meant points would be at a premium.

Qualification for the second group phase had not only boosted the Elland Road coffers, it had also stoked the fires of ambition in the boardroom. The build-up to the visit of Real Madrid centred on Leeds trying to prise Rio Ferdinand away from West Ham with a world record £18 million bid. Just a few short years ago Leeds' idea of a new signing was someone who had once played for either Sheffield Wednesday or United and had reached what is politely known as 'the veteran stage'. Or what was known on the Kop as being shit. The likes of Nigel Worthington, John Pemberton and Mark Beesley could never be faulted for effort, but they were also hardly the signings on which to build our golden future. Every time Howard Wilkinson made another signing in the mid-1990s, the club seemed to take a step back. Ferdinand was different and the attempt to sign such a talented player, allied to the boost of qualifying for this stage, meant we approached Elland Road full of renewed hope ahead of the clash with Real Madrid.

Excited talk filled the night as we walked across the footbridge that runs over the M621 just five minutes from the stadium.

"The atmosphere will be something special tonight. Real Madrid might play in front of 90,000 Spaniards every week, but they won't have heard anything like us tonight."

"An early goal like we got against Barcelona will put the wind up 'em."

I had again passed the afternoon with Drew before making my way to The Britannia about an hour before kick-off. We bumped into the Doctor and, as Drew had never met him before, he listened intently to his tales from the past.

I've heard most of them at least three times, but I still fall about when the Doctor reminisces about a pre-season trip to Germany a few years back. He had enjoyed a few drinks before the friendly and decided it would be a good idea to mount a one man pitch invasion. The fact that play was still going on was funny enough, but the Doctor being as naked as the day he was born brought the house down as the crowd cheered his every move. Unfortunately, it did not have a happy ending for the Doctor.

His Mum, who is German, was staying with friends in a nearby town, and when the Doctor spoke to her the next day she asked him how the match had gone.

"Fine, Mum. It was quite a good game."

"I heard there was a streaker who ran on the pitch during the game."

The Doctor acted all innocent as he said, "Was there?"

His Mum wasn't fooled though. "I'm surprised you don't know anything about it. There is a photo of this streaker on the front page of this morning's paper and, unless I am very much mistaken, it is you running around with no clothes on! What were you thinking of? I'm so ashamed."

The Doctor, suitably shame-faced, apologised to his Mum and kept a low profile for the rest of the tour.

Walking through the turnstiles to enter the Kop ahead of the Real Madrid game, we wondered how many visiting supporters would have travelled from the Spanish capital. We soon got our answer. Sat in just one section of seats in the top tier of the South Stand were around 125 away fans. It was a pathetic turnout for the reigning European champions although poor away supports would be a recurring theme at Elland Road all season. Barcelona brought a similar amount as their great rivals, while Lazio's travelling 'army' numbered just six - maybe the first case of an away support actually arriving in a taxi!

Roared on by a passionate crowd, Leeds did well in the first half with Jonathan Woodgate hitting the post with a close-range shot. Real Madrid managed just a couple of half-hearted efforts.

At half-time I bumped into the Doctor again in the concourse underneath the Kop. The previous night, Manchester United had been played off the park by Panathinaikos, but still managed to win 3-1 thanks to two late goals. The Doctor was still fuming as he launched into a tirade against all things Manc. He hates them with a passion, but there is a sure-fire way to take the wind out of his sails whenever he starts a rant about Manchester United.

The flight home from Prague after a UEFA Cup quarter-final the previous season had seen us travel with Go!, a budget airline that was then a part of British Airways. As ever, the noise level had risen by about 20 decibels when the Doctor had taken his seat on the front row of the plane. Halfway through the flight, one of the stewardesses announced that the duty frees would soon be on sale, but it was her final line which left the Doctor, for the first time in living memory, speechless.

"Quite a few famous people have flown with Go! recently and just last week we had Posh Spice on here. She was sat down here in the front row in that very seat."

As the stewardess pointed at the Doctor, his face dropped. The front five rows of the plane dissolved into uncontrollable laughter at the irony that the wife of David Beckham, the player he hates more than any other, had been sat in his very seat. The Doctor was immediately re-christened 'Scunny Spice' and to this day he has vowed never to fly with Go! again.

Returning to my seat for the start of the second half, I was hoping for more of the same from Leeds. Unfortunately, Real's quality started to shine through and goals from Fernando Hierra and Raul gave the Spanish club a deserved 2-0 win.

At the final whistle, we gave both sides a warm round of applause. The better side had beaten us and there was no disgrace in that.

In the night's other opening game in Group D, a superb individual goal from Tomasz Radzinski was enough to give Anderlecht a shock 1-0 victory over Lazio in Brussels. That left us bottom of the group after one game and meant we needed to get a point in our next outing against Lazio to realistically keep our hopes of qualifying alive.

* * *

Rome is one of my favourite cities in Europe. I had enjoyed spending a few days in the 'Eternal City' the previous March and vowed then that I would return. I now had my wish. With Christmas being just a few weeks away, it was clear there would be nothing like the numbers that travelled to Milan. Whitby John was going though and rang with good news.

"I've just been on the internet and can get flights to the west coast of Italy for £4 return!"

"Four quid? How the hell do the airline make any money on that?"

"Who cares? They've made enough out of us over the years. We will have to pay the airport tax and that will make it £13. Rome is only an hour away by train. Are you in?"

It was tempting, but I was struggling for time off so decided to travel with the club on the official one day trip. At £229 it was a lot more expensive than Whitby John's route, but I would be there and back in one day. It was settled that I would meet Whitby John and the Doctor in a bar behind the Termini main train station at two-thirty on the afternoon of the game.

I was travelling out on my own but, as with most trips, I soon bumped into a couple of familiar faces. One of these was Billy, a Leeds fan I had first met in Milan and subsequently bumped into a week later after United had beaten Arsenal 1-0 at Elland Road. I was halfway through my first pint in the Yorkshire Heroes bar at Leeds-Bradford Airport when he ambled over. He was also travelling on his own so we decided to tour round Rome together before meeting Whitby John and the Doctor.

Rome is a vast city although the historic centre is relatively small. It stretches from the Villa Borghese, a park area to the north, to Palatino (Palatine Hill) to the south, and from the twisting Tiber river in the west to the Termini in the east. The Vatican, which boasts its own postal service, newspaper, currency and army of Swiss Guards, lies just across the Tiber from the historic centre.

The previous March, we had spent three days in Rome and soon found out the best way to enjoy the city was on foot. There is so much to see in the historic centre that no matter how long you spend in Rome, it won't be enough. I have now been twice, but don't feel to have even scratched the surface.

Time was at a premium ahead of the game so Bill and I decided the Colosseum was the sight-seeing priority. Nine months earlier, I had caught only a fleeting glimpse of this amazing structure from the back of a taxi, and having since watched the excellent *Gladiator* film starring Russell Crowe I was determined to do better this time around.

We touched down in Rome mid-morning, but a rather over-the-top police escort meant we didn't arrive at Villa Borghese until around 1pm. A quick metro trip later and we were stood in the shadow of the Colosseum.

Once inside, it is easy to imagine what the 2,000 year old structure looked like in its heyday. It must have been an amazing place to watch the gladiator combat with the defeated warriors often paying the ultimate price with their life.

"A bit like going to Millwall in the 1980s," was how Billy summed it up.

Once back in the city centre, we met Whitby John and the Doctor who had enjoyed a good night in a coastal town before travelling to

74

Rome that morning. They had found a hotel for £12 a night and were pleased with their work. The afternoon was passed moving from bar to bar, but we didn't see any other Leeds fans until about 6pm when we walked into the Twins Bar.

On most of our European trips, there is a bar where everyone congregates. To an outsider, it must look pre-arranged and confirm the fallacy often promoted by the press that large groups of English football fans are controlled by some 'General' type figure. The trouble that occurred in Euro 2000 and France '98, we were reliably told by the press, was organised by 'a disciplined group of English trouble-makers hell-bent on causing violence'. Just how disciplined anyone can be after spending hours drinking strong lager in the sun, as the vast majority did in Charleroi and Marseille, is strangely enough ignored by these very same newspapers.

The fact is fans tend to gravitate towards the same area on Euro aways and therefore one bar does become the focus for people meeting up. Situated directly behind the Termini, the Twins Bar was just such a place in Rome when Leeds were in town. It had been packed out from early morning to late at night in the days surrounding Leeds' previous two visits to Rome. We had got to know the two brothers who ran the bar nine months earlier, but I didn't expect them to remember us. But the moment we walked through the door one of them ran up and planted a kiss on each of our cheeks before saying, "Great to see you boys – welcome back!"

He had been hoping we would pop in because he had bought a video presented by former Leeds midfielder, Vinnie Jones. It featured clips of violent incidents in matches around the world ranging from mass brawls involving players to even a referee knocking out someone protesting at a decision. We passed an hour watching this video, cheering as each clip got more and more absurd. Andy, a Leeds fan from London, arrived in the bar with a couple of mates who supported Grimsby but had come along to enjoy a few days in Rome. We were the first Leeds fans Andy had seen all day.

"I can't believe the contrast with our last visit. Last time we came to Rome, you couldn't walk five yards without hearing another rendition of *Marching On Together*."

Earlier in the day, a bar owner had warned Andy to be careful at the Olympic Stadium later that night because Lazio fans had one of the worst reputations in Italy. It is the sort of scare-mongering heard when abroad, but with several Leeds fans being stabbed before the Roma game earlier in the year, we would be taking no chances.

Eventually, the time came for us to head off to the ground, and because we had left it late a taxi seemed the best option. Unsurprisingly, stopping for four English football fans did not seem too attractive an option for Rome's taxi drivers as they sailed straight past. After about 15 minutes, we were just about to give up when a taxi slowed so we jumped in. I have caught my fair share of taxis in European cities and the one constant is they will try and rip you off. However, in Rome it was not being cheated out of some lira that bothered us. Instead, it was whether we would actually reach the stadium alive. I have never been as frightened in my life as I was during the 15 minute drive. I don't think he used the brakes once and this despite the rest of the traffic travelling at about 20mph. We never dipped below 40mph as he swerved from lane to lane and round queuing cars. At one stage, we even mounted the pavement, which came as something of a shock to the people walking on it.

"Use your brakes you silly bastard," was the Doctor's advice, but the driver either didn't speak English or chose to ignore us.

After our fifth near miss in two minutes, the driver started laughing manically as though he was having the time of his life. We weren't and thankfully it was soon over. Whitby John and the Doctor went off looking for one last drink, but I wanted to get inside. Our tickets were for the opposite end of the stadium from where we had been stood against Roma so we decided to follow the stadium round to the right. Big mistake! We ended up walking up the hill and a stroll that should have taken five minutes, instead took us 20. Eventually, we arrived at the turnstiles to be met by hundreds of carabinieri, the military police in Italy.

The Leeds United Travel staff had warned us on the plane journey from England that cameras, mobile phones, belts and coins would all be confiscated by the police to prevent them being used as missiles. Leaving aside the fact that we would have to be the most affluent fans in Europe if we could afford to throw away phones or cameras, it also turned out that anyone who did want to launch such a valuable item would have to be an Olympic standard thrower due to the Lazio fans being 50 yards away. I opted to hide my phone down my trousers while Billy went one better in stashing his loose change in a bush near the turnstiles. He later reclaimed the money as we left the stadium.

Once inside, I saw Andy who had also caught a taxi from the Twins Bar to the stadium and he looked to be in shock.

"We were walking round the outside when these Italians ran at us and one of them knocked me down with some sort of martial arts chain. Thankfully, I was next to a turnstile manned by stewards and they came out to rescue me. My head is bloody killing me though!"

With both Leeds and Lazio having lost their opening game, this was a match neither side could afford to lose. I therefore felt the Stadio Olimpico would be packed, but instead just 26,000 turned up, including around 800 Leeds fans.

Our seats were perched high in the Curva Sud with hundreds of unsmiling police surrounding us, many tapping rather menacingly on their batons. The stadium also has a track surrounding the pitch, which means we were quite a way from the action. The fire brigade pour gallons of water on to it before every game to prevent flares thrown from the crowd setting it alight.

The vast majority of the home fans were sat at the opposite end where the odd abusive banner could be seen. It always amuses me to see the home fans go to such trouble to create a banner in English when we come to town. I couldn't ever imagine one appearing at Elland Road questioning Figo's parentage in Portuguese.

Much of the pre-match focus had been on the racist reputation of the Lazio supporters. The club has had a right wing support for many years, but the abuse heaped on Arsenal's Patrick Vieira in a European tie a few weeks earlier had brought a long overdue reaction from UEFA who ordered Lazio to clean up their act. Lazio's Sinisa Mihajlovic had even racially abused Vieira during the game and although the Yugoslav initially apologised, he later retracted it. Olivier Dacourt, a friend of Vieira, had said he would kick Mihajlovic if he was abused during the match and it was clear we could be in for a real battle. I just hoped the referee would be strong.

A bookmaker back home had priced Leeds at 6-1, but I still wasn't tempted to put a few quid on the lads. The best I was hoping for was a draw. As the players lined up for kick-off, the home fans tried to drown out our efforts by whistling and jeering, but it didn't faze us.

"Rule Britannia, Britannia rules the waves,

Britons never, never, never shall be slaves!"

The early play was scrappy which left Whitby John unimpressed. "We shouldn't be scared of this lot, they are no better than us."

We had a couple of narrow escapes in the first half, while at the other end, Lee Bowyer came within inches of giving us the lead when he struck a post.

The futility of confiscating coins and cameras at the turnstiles was proved during the half-time break as any fan paying for a drink or a bite to eat was given their change in, yes you've guessed it, coins. The pre-match suspicion that the police had been collecting for their Christmas party seemed just about right.

The second 45 minutes was the best I had seen Leeds play in a long time. We dominated Lazio, but still the goal wouldn't come.

"How many more fucking chances are we going to squander?" asked Whitby John.

It seemed like being one of those nights where the ball just wouldn't go in. The arrival of Harry Kewell off the bench with just 14 minutes left changed all that though. Within a couple of minutes, Kewell collected the ball wide on the left and after playing the ball in to Alan Smith, the young striker found Mark Viduka. The big Aussie controlled the ball and, spotting Smith continuing his run into the penalty area, he deftly back-heeled a pass into his team-mate's path. Perched high in the stand behind the goal, time appeared to stand still as Peruzzi rushed from his line to try to block Smith. I always wonder what goes through a player's mind at such a time. Does he have time to decide whether to place a shot or just crack it and hope for the best? Or does instinct take over?

Smith looked up quickly and, cool as you like, simply rolled the ball past Peruzzi and into the net. A quick look back to ensure he was not offside and then Smith ran to the far touchline before being mobbed by elated team-mates. The scenes in the away enclosure were of sheer pandemonium. I hugged and was hugged. Like Milan, it was a moment when I lost myself and had no control over my actions.

I always feel sorry for people who say they don't follow a football team. No matter how great their life is, I don't think they ever experience the feeling of pure elation of the seconds that follow a vital goal like Smithy's. Maybe shagging Liz Hurley would come close, but even then I'm not too sure. And that is what I love about football. I have many miserable memories of watching Leeds. Losing 3-2 at home to Shrewsbury in the last minute after being 2-0 down at half-time is one. So is getting knocked out of the League Cup by Mansfield. And Portsmouth, Oxford, Reading and Wolves in the FA Cup. But it is those experiences that make moments like Smith's winning goal in Rome all the more memorable. You have to suffer the lows to really appreciate the highs.

Lazio tried to grab an equaliser, but Leeds stood firm. This was our night and nothing was going to spoil it. The final whistle soon blew to prompt more celebratory scenes among the travelling fans. Our heroes swapped shirts with their crest-fallen opponents before running over to celebrate in front of us. Within a couple of minutes, the players were filing back to the dressing room and Peter Ridsdale took centre stage as he applauded us from the track. We wanted the players back out to celebrate yet another famous night in Europe.

"Ridsdale, get the team!

Ridsdale, Ridsdale get the team!"

The Leeds chairman gave us the thumbs-up and disappeared back to the dressing room. A couple of minutes later, he was back and shouted up that the players would be out as soon as possible. In the meantime, Ridsdale asked for quiet before launching his own rendition of *Marching On Together*. Just like in Milan, we needed no invitation to join in and duly sang the club's anthem with a passion that seemed to surprise the few Lazio fans still in the stadium.

Again, like in the San Siro, Gary Kelly led the way but this time his team-mates were asked to join in. Our first appeal was for Smithy to give us a song. The young striker stepped forward, clutching his Burberry bootbag, and asked for quiet.

"Y – R – A. We're Yorkshire's Republican Army, we're barmy,

Wherever we go, we fear no foe, for we are the YRA!"

In the 1980s, most club's hooligans gave themselves a name with the likes of the ICF (Inter-City Firm) of West Ham and the Chelsea Headhunters. Some names were plain daft with the Birmingham Zulu Warriors probably my favourite. Leeds had The Service Crew until around 1987 and then the tag YRA was adopted.

"I wonder if Smithy will start singing about The Service Crew next," laughed Whitby John.

Rio Ferdinand, who had signed a week earlier but was ineligible to play until after Christmas, was the next to step forward which prompted someone to shout, "Don't you dare sing *I'm Forever Blowing Bubbles*, Rio!"

The England defender managed just the words "Marching on" before being drowned out by 800 backing singers.

After his embarrassment in Milan when trying to sing a song even his team-mates didn't understand, Lee Bowyer played it safe with a rousing "Let's go fucking mental!", while Harry Kewell chipped in with "Glory, Glory Leeds United!!"

The team finally made their way out of the stadium, but we weren't so lucky as the police kept us in another half-hour. No-one cared though as we treated the empty stadium to even more of the United back catalogue of songs. I went to sit on the back row of the away enclosure just so I could take in the sight. I wanted to savour every second because moments like this don't come along too often for Leeds fans. The following Saturday we lost at Southampton so I was glad I did take time to step back and take in what was happening around me.

Eventually, we were allowed to leave. The police had long since relaxed and seemed to quite enjoy our post-match karaoke session with the players. Some Leeds fans even shook hands with the police while singing "There's only one carabinieri!" as they filed out of the stadium.

The coaches to transport us back to the airport were waiting directly outside the exit so in a matter of minutes we were heading away from the Stadio Olimpico in triumphant mood.

Real Madrid had thrashed Anderlecht 4-1 in the Bernabeu so Leeds were second on goal difference. The victory had left us in a strong position with qualification back in our own hands.

That didn't matter tonight though as the plane brought us home. This was a night to celebrate one result, not look ahead to facing Anderlecht in ten weeks time when the competition resumed. Leeds had conquered Rome and I for one wanted to savour every moment of a very special night.

Chapter Seven

Whingeing Belgians

Life as a football fan today is very different to that in the 1980s. Back then, we were hated by the police, tolerated at best by the clubs, and shunned by much of society. In many eyes, muttering the words "I support Leeds United," was akin to saying "I mug old ladies." We were scum, end of story.

Fast forward to the 21st Century and everything has changed. The middle classes have adopted 'footie', a word I detest almost as much as the American 'soccer', with the world and his wife now wanting to discuss the merits of Sven-Goran Eriksson, David Beckham and Michael Owen.

Many things have changed for the better. The days of my shoes being covered in piss as the rain caused the urinals in the open air toilets at Birmingham to overflow once again are long gone. So is standing out in the open at places like Oldham and Crystal Palace, shivering as Leeds slumped to defeat. Getting from Old Trafford to Piccadilly Station is still a bit hairy today after visiting the Theatre of Wet Dreams with Leeds, but in the main, away trips are now hassle-free.

Unfortunately, one area that has not improved is the atmosphere inside the grounds. In the 1980s, 15,000 made twice as much noise inside Elland Road as 40,000 manage now. The abolition of the terraces is a huge contributing factor.

When Leeds were in the old Second Division, I used to stand at the back of the Kop, on the left side. If you wanted a decent vantage point then you had to get there a good 45 minutes before kick-off. That, in turn, meant the atmosphere built up gradually with most players receiving a name-check while warming up. Now, anyone arriving 45 minutes before kick-off is treated to deafening music and a DJ who seems to think no-one will understand him unless he shouts at the top of his voice. Leeds also have their very own mascot, Ellie The Elephant, who walks around entertaining the kids. As mascots go, Ellie is not too bad and definitely a step up from Bradford City who have a middle-aged man walking round in a pair of tight shorts while handing sweets out to children – hardly the best image for football!

The visit of Manchester United apart, Elland Road is rarely a seething cauldron of passion in the Premiership, but European nights are different. As soon as the teams walk out of the tunnel, it is clear we are in for a very special evening. The resumption of our Champions League campaign brought Anderlecht to West Yorkshire and the atmosphere was electric.

Since the famous win in Rome ten weeks earlier, we had managed to turn our domestic season round. A goalless draw at home to Derby the previous Saturday had been disappointing, but the point was enough to lift Leeds into fifth place. Just a month earlier, we'd been 14th in the Premiership and our only possible route to Europe looked like being via the much-maligned Inter Toto Cup. This was something I was desperate to avoid because I had spent the previous summer telling Bradford City fans who were watching their team compete in the Inter Toto for the first time, what a Mickey Mouse tournament it was. I wasn't over keen on the sarcastic "So it's good enough now then, is it?" phone calls from Bradford-supporting friends.

Thankfully victories over Coventry, Aston Villa, Manchester City and Ipswich had changed that thinking and I was now looking forward to a double-header with Anderlecht full of renewed confidence.

We were set to play Anderlecht at Elland Road on the Tuesday with the return leg taking place in Belgium eight days later. Two victories for us allied with two defeats for Lazio against Real Madrid would put us through, but such thoughts were so fanciful that we dismissed them on the afternoon of the home tie. Four points would be a great return and leave us probably needing to beat Lazio in the final group game to progress to the quarter-finals.

Superstition undoubtedly plays a large part in football with some players insisting they be the last out of the tunnel while others will put their left boot on first. Supporters are no different. Ahead of the home ties with Barcelona, Besiktas and 1860 Munich, I had passed an enjoyable hour or so in Bradford catching up with old workmates during their lunch hours. The home clash with Real Madrid had been the only time I hadn't been in Bradford earlier in the day and with Leeds losing 2-0 it meant a new superstition had been born. The lunchtime of the Anderlecht home tie was therefore duly spent in Bradford with Drew before making the short ten mile journey to Leeds by train.

Leeds' results had certainly picked up in the past month, but unfortunately the scoring records of our two main strikers had not. Alan Smith went into the Anderlecht tie having scored just once in four months while Mark Viduka boasted one goal in two months. Leeds fans love a trier and that is why Smithy is rarely criticised at Elland Road. You can see that, as a Leeds fan, he wants to win just as much as we do. If any of us had been lucky enough to play for Leeds, we would play like Smithy. Or David Batty. The fact Leeds fans love a trier was illustrated in the home game with Sunderland before Christmas when Harry Kewell and Batty were both making their first appearances of the season at Elland Road following injury. Kewell is rightly hailed as one of the best talents in Europe, but his reception was muted from the Kop compared to that given to substitute Batty who was cheered wildly every time he ran up and down the touchline.

Viduka, meanwhile, had come in for criticism from a section of the Leeds fans. The big Aussie is a tremendously skilful player, but his laid-back playing style had led to some accusing him of a lack of effort. In the eyes of Leeds' fans there can be no bigger crime, and in the two previous games against Derby and Everton, many had turned on Viduka. I felt it unfair. There have been some players who were not fit to wear the Leeds shirt – for some reason, the name Carlton Palmer springs to mind – but Viduka is a superb player whose style dove-tails perfectly with Smithy's all-action efforts. I knew that a couple of goals from the Aussie and all would be forgiven in the fans' eyes so tonight could be a big one for him.

Anderlecht's visit to Old Trafford had seen them crash 5-1 to Manchester United back in September, but it was the behaviour of their fans that had raised eyebrows. On the morning of the match, a group of Belgian fans had thrown missiles at workers arriving at their offices and there were a number of incidents later in the day.

In Leeds, the Belgians were out as early as 8.30am in City Square where they sat around drinking cans of Stella. There were rumours of trouble being planned up near the Merrion Centre, but the day passed off quietly.

Anderlecht's record of having won every game, including four Champions League ties, at their compact Stade Constant Vanden Stock home meant we had to win at Elland Road. Anything less would leave us struggling. Anderlecht's golden period was undoubtedly the early 1980s, although the side's achievements in winning the UEFA Cup, finishing as losing finalists and reaching two European Cup semi-finals have been tainted since by a bribery scandal.

After winning the UEFA Cup in 1983, the Belgians were drawn against Nottingham Forest in the semi-final of the following year's competition. A 2-0 victory for Forest at The City Ground caused panic at the Brussels club as the money spent on stadium redevelopment had to be recouped with a lucrative final appearance. The referee in the second leg, which Anderlecht won 3-0 with Forest having a blatant penalty turned down and a goal disallowed, has since died, but then club president, Constant Vanden Stock, admitted in 1997 that he had bribed the official. Spurs beat the Belgians in the two-legged final, but Anderlecht's stadium had been filled one additional time.

A European Cup semi-final defeat by Steaua Bucharest in 1986 and a Cup Winners' Cup final reverse against Sampdoria apart, Anderlecht's European record since the Spurs final loss has been undistinguished.

But a convincing 3-1 win over Manchester United in Brussels in the first group phase illustrated that the Belgians are again emerging as a force in Europe. We knew it would be tough so we sang our hearts out in the hope we could lift the team.

Every tackle was cheered wildly while a threatening attack drew a huge roar from the capacity crowd. Smithy floored Viduka as the pair stretched to reach Lee Bowyer's cross early in the game and although it was the youngster who was at fault, this did not stop the Aussie being criticised by several fans around me on the Kop.

"Buck your ideas up you lazy sod!"

"Get Harry Kewell on instead of that idle bastard!"

If that was the reaction to the Aussie being felled by a team-mate, I was dreading what would happen if Viduka actually had the temerity to miss a chance.

After the initial threat from both sides, the first half soon settled down, but the volume of noise from the stands was maintained.

At half-time, I had to meet Whitby John to pay the balance of the trip to Madrid. Stood in the concourse underneath the Kop, most people agreed the points would be ours if we could move up a gear. The arrival of Harry Kewell off the bench just nine minutes into the second half lifted those hopes. Typically, the Belgians promptly took the lead. Stoics collected the ball on the edge of the penalty area and after a neat one–two with Goor, the Romanian international ran on to coolly roll the ball past Nigel Martyn.

The 1,200 away fans celebrated while we stood in silence. We needed a lift and thankfully it came in the 75th minute through Ian Harte. Earlier in the season, the Republic Of Ireland left back had produced some dreadful free-kicks with most flying yards wide of the target. However, a goal the previous midweek at Everton in a 2-2 draw had boosted his confidence, so when Leeds won a free-kick 25 yards from the Belgians' goal, we offered our support.

"Ian Harte, Harte Harte!

Ian Harte, Harte Harte!"

Anderlecht keeper, Zvonko Milojevic, bizarrely chose to put just three men in the wall and Harte had his chance. After carefully positioning the ball and stepping back a couple of yards, Harte ran up and curled a left-foot shot over the wall and into the corner of the net. Cue celebrations of both joy and relief. We were back in it.

The stunned looks of disappointment on the faces of the visiting players as they trudged back to the centre-circle told their own story. They knew a torrid 15 minutes awaited them as Leeds chased a winner.

Koller had a golden chance to settle his side's nerves, but he missed an open goal. Maybe it was destined to be our night after all? There were four minutes left on the clock when we got our answer.

A long punt upfield fell kindly for Aleksander Illic midway inside his own half only for the defender to inexplicably tread on the ball. Smith was alert and sent an inch-perfect pass through for Lee Bowyer as he raced into the penalty area. I held my breath on the Kop. Our whole season rested on this moment. Miss it and I was sure qualification would be beyond us. Score, and we had to be favourites.

The ball looked to be running away from Bowyer, but at the vital time he stretched out his right foot to wrap it round the ball and drill it towards goal. I was stood directly behind the path of the ball, but it seemed to be travelling in slow motion as the keeper went down to try to block the effort. Milojevic was a fraction too late and the ball ran sweetly between his legs and into the net. Goal!

Bowyer ran to celebrate with the Kop, but only got about three strides before he was submerged by equally delighted team-mates. All around Elland Road, the joy was unconfined. Friends and strangers yelled, jumped up and down and hugged like there was no tomorrow. From being one goal down with just 15 minutes remaining, we were now ahead. The game restarted, and although Martyn had to again be alert to deny Walter Baseggio in stoppage time, it was soon all over. We had another three vital points and celebrated accordingly while the Belgians slumped to the ground.

Bitter visiting coach Aime Anthuenis, no doubt chomping on a bunch of sour grapes at the time, said, "Leeds are not a good side. I was not at all impressed with them. How can a home team create so few chances and win the game? From what I have seen here we have nothing to fear in Brussels next week."

Reading the following day's papers I thought it was a very kind gesture from the Belgian to give David O'Leary some assistance with his team-talk ahead of the return game. So thank you Mr Anthuenis, we salute you!

More carping from the whingeing Belgians dominated the build-up to the return eight days later. Having French midfielder Olivier Dacourt in the squad meant the United squad had someone who could translate what the Anderlecht players were saying in their local press. And none of it was too complimentary about David O'Leary and his team.

Brussels was one of the easier trips to make following Leeds abroad with many opting for the cheaper option of Eurostar, which runs direct to Brussels from London.

I plumped for Brussels while Whitby John, the Doctor and Tally all opted for a couple of days in nearby Antwerp. Their decision turned out to be the smarter one with Antwerp being something of a party city with the bars open all night. Brussels, in contrast, seems to shut down at 2am with even most of the late night takeaways shutting their doors early. The police in the Belgian capital also seem to treat English football fans with the courtesy usually reserved for muggers and rapists. We weren't welcome.

The city is situated at the crossroads of Europe, with London, Paris, Amsterdam and Cologne all similar distances away. It is also home to the European Union. The centre of Brussels is divided into the upper and lower town with the latter being based loosely around the imposing Grand Place, a former market square that visitors tend to gravitate towards. This is a pleasant area to amble round during the day with popular pavement cafes in the shadow of the towering Hotel de Ville. A perfect place to stop and watch the world go by, even in February.

The Grand Place lies just five minutes walk from the main road, Boulevard Anspach, which runs through the city centre. After Euro 2000, when English fans were attacked and deported indiscriminately by the local police, most Leeds fans had opted to stay outside Brussels, with Antwerp, Bruges and Amsterdam all preferred bases. Therefore, as I walked round the city centre on the evening before the game there were very few familiar faces around.

After laughing at Manchester United's Wes Brown putting through his own goal to give Valencia a 1-1 draw at Old Trafford in O'Reilly's Irish Bar, I joined my mate Simon in a wander from bar to bar for a couple of hours. Unknowingly, we wandered rather too far and ended up in the streets around the Gare du Nord train station, an area renowned as the Turkish quarters. We had one drink in a dingy bar, but soon realised that we weren't too welcome so left quickly and hailed a passing taxi. We clambered in and moments later the occupants of the bar came charging out. It didn't look like a friendly discussion of the following night's game was on their minds so we urged the taxi driver to put his foot down. A lucky escape.

The Belgian press had challenged their English counterparts to a game of football on the day of the Anderlecht-Leeds game, and before leaving England I had rather foolishly agreed to play. It was a decision I regretted the moment my alarm rang. After the near escape of the previous evening, we had retreated to the hotel bar and stayed up rather longer than is advisable when playing football the next day.

Looking at the state of the English press in their hotel reception, they had enjoyed a similar evening sampling the strong Belgian beer. I knew playing football was a bad idea, but *The Daily*

Telegraph's Henry Winter had brought the kit so the game was on. The fact it was the England away kit should have told me to stay away, red never having been my favourite colour for obvious reasons.

The game was being staged at Anderlecht's training ground, and on arrival in a fleet of taxis, it looked a decent playing surface and even had a stand down one side of the pitch. The Belgians were obviously taking this game seriously as there was a qualified referee and two linesmen waiting as well.

Team boss Ian Edwards of *The Mirror* revealed the team with 'Peter' (my nickname - as in Peter Sutcliffe) pencilled in as right back. When playing for my college team, I had been an overlapping right back, but the intervening years had turned me into just a right back. Forays down the right flank were definitely not on the agenda in Belgium.

The opening minute set the tone for the 89 that would follow as no less than three English players mis-controlled the ball. Within five minutes we were behind and struggling. The Belgians rather cunningly passed to their own side, while we, in true English style, lumped it 50 yards down the pitch.

The sweat poured off me and I swear it tasted of Stella Artois. Soon it was 2-0 and I had suffered enough so asked to come off. *The Daily Star*'s Simon Mullock then clattered an opponent out of the game with a dreadful tackle to leave one of the Belgians protesting, "It is only a game."

He was met with the reply of "Piss off!", but before half-time it was 3-0. Unfortunately, our humiliation was not complete.

With one Belgian already out of the game and two others having to leave early for work, the home side played with eight men for the second 45 minutes and still scored twice. I came back on and played up front with Henry Winter for the final 30 minutes, but, alas, we could not find that elusive goal. In fact, I must have been caught offside 15 times during that spell. The Times' *Matt Dickinson*, the man who conducted the interview with Glenn Hoddle that brought about the end of his spell as England boss, was not a happy man and vowed "to do one of these cocky Belgians."

Unfortunately, the home team were far too quick and it was a thoroughly humiliated English press team that trooped from the field. Back in the dressing room, it was decided that not a word of this abject 5-0 defeat would be uttered to the rest of the press, but unfortunately word spread fast. Norman Hunter was the first person we met back in the city centre.

"Eight men? What the hell were you doing?"

Our cover was blown. We had no alternative but to hold our hands up and admit the Belgians were better than us. I just hoped it wasn't an omen. A point would be a great result for Leeds, especially with the proud home record Anderlecht boasted.

The Belgian police force must have had all leave cancelled judging by the number of officers on the streets of Brussels during the afternoon as I wandered round. Water cannon were also strategically located throughout the city and it left you wondering just who they were expecting to be travelling from England. The police presence outside the stadium was just as over-the-top with an unbelievably large amount of officers looking on as 1,300 Leeds fans went through the turnstiles.

Redeveloped in the early 1980s, the Constant Vanden Stock Stadium is a modern smart stadium that has two tiers of seats on all four sides. Intimate without being intimidating, it has nevertheless proved to be a fortress for the home side. The Leeds section covered about a third of one end of the stadium with supporters in both tiers. The price for the upper tier was an unbelievable £50 with my ticket in the lower tier costing £10 less. The segregation in that lower tier amounted to a Perspex wall measuring about seven feet in height. However, with no stewards or police present, it allowed both sets of fans to taunt each other freely in the build-up to kick-off.

As the game developed, it was us who did more of the taunting. Marl Viduka did superbly on the left to create space to cross the ball for Alan Smith to drill into the net for our first goal. The celebrations were still continuing when Dominic Matteo's cross picked out Viduka and he nodded the ball over the home keeper. 2-0 up but the best was still to come.

A wonderful move involving David Batty and Viduka allowed Smithy to charge through before chipping the ball wonderfully over the keeper and into the net. Three goals up and it wasn't even half-time! We couldn't let the chance pass to gloat at the Anderlecht coach's expense.

"We're shit, but we're 3-0 up! We're shit, but we're 3-0 up!"

The home fans' English was obviously a lot better than my French because they weren't too chuffed and reacted by banging on the Perspex wall. We just held up three fingers and started singing "Can we play you every week?" which upset them even more.

The freakish Jan Koller pulled a goal back with 15 minutes left, but this couldn't dampen our spirits. Ian Harte made it 4-1 from the penalty spot, which left us anxious to hear how Lazio-Real Madrid had finished. We didn't have long to wait and it was the best news possible. The game in the Olimpico Stadio had finished level and that meant, unbelievably, we were through with two games to spare. Manchester United and Arsenal still had a lot of work to do so we were the only English side already through. That just made the feeling sweeter.

20 minutes after the final whistle and we were still being held in the ground when the Belgian police formed a line of officers across the centre of the pitch. With all the home fans long gone, it was one of the most pointless acts I've seen and drew a predictable response of "Who the fucking hell are you?" from the Leeds fans.

Tally, Whitby John and Doctor Who returned to Antwerp, which left the rest of us in Brussels. After Milan in the first group phase, I had been too tired to celebrate properly so was determined to make up for it in Belgium.

Unfortunately, Brussels shut down soon after midnight with just a couple of late night bars providing us with a few welcome beers. After a fruitless search for some action, we decided to call it a night with a takeaway burger before retiring to the hotel. It had been an amazing night when Leeds had again proved we are an emerging force in European football.

The trip to Madrid in a fortnight's time would now be a relaxing few days free from the stress and worry of how Leeds would fare in the Bernabeu. We could now sit back and relax while hoping Manchester United would come a cropper in their final two group games.

Chapter Eight

The Hand Of Sod

I have lost count of the number of kick-offs I have missed over the years. I once went through a full season, our first back in Division One after promotion in 1990, without being inside Elland Road when a game started. Away games are even worse. The last time I made it in for kick-off without a late dash was at Spurs in May, 1995, and that was only because the police rounded all Leeds fans up at St Pancras Station before escorting us via the tube to White Hart Lane. I was sat in my seat about 45 minutes before kick-off and was so bored I vowed never to be in so early again.

The shortest time I have spent in a football ground is two minutes (and that included a visit to the Gents). An away day in London had left us slightly the worse for wear and we didn't arrive at Stamford Bridge until the game was 40 minutes old. We sat down to learn Leeds were 3-0 down to Chelsea and that we were "playing shit", according to the bloke sat to my left. The first piece of action we saw was Carlton Palmer hoofing the ball straight into touch. We'd seen enough and promptly stood up and walked straight back out again. Leeds eventually lost 4-1 while we returned to Covent Garden for a few more drinks so I think we made the right choice.

Compared to Alec, however, I have an unblemished record. The week before we were due to fly to Madrid, Leeds had been playing at Spurs. No-one had seen Alec after 2pm on that day so Whitby John asked what had happened.

"I had a right day. I got to London and went for a drink in King's Cross with you lot. I had a few and then the next few hours are a blur. The next thing I remember is getting my hair cut somewhere in King's Cross about half-six and then having a few more drinks. I eventually missed the train back to Doncaster and the furthest north I could get was Kettering."

"How the hell did you get home from there?"

'A taxi that cost me £100. All in all, I spent about £250 and didn't get within five miles of Spurs. I found my unused ticket the next day when I emptied my pockets."

We all fell about laughing. We were stood outside Elland Road about half an hour before Leeds were set to play Manchester United. We were due to fly to Madrid from Manchester Airport straight after the game.

I love playing Manchester United, or 'Scum' as they are affectionately known round our way, because it is the only time the atmosphere inside Elland Road approaches what it was like in the 1980s for a League game. The mutual hatred from both sets of supporters always ensures this is a fixture we love to win. We should have beaten them as well only for a linesman to wrongly rule Wes Brown's own goal out for offside so the scores finished level at 1-1. The disappointment was quickly forgotten though as we looked forward to four days in Spain.

Whitby John had organised the trip for 40 of us. Because we needed to be at the airport later that same afternoon, a coach was organised to transport us across the Pennines. We were told it would be waiting for us at the end of the game, but it was nowhere to be seen.

A frantic call to the coach company saw Whitby John told, "The coach is there. You can't be looking very hard."

Three of us went round the coach park, but still there was no sign. Out came Whitby John's mobile again.

"I have just spoken to the driver and he says he can see the Billy Bremner statue on the corner of Lowfields Road and Elland Road."

The penny suddenly dropped.

"He can't be parked with the Scum coaches!"

Unfortunately, he was. As cock-ups go, this was a big one. By now, the visiting fans had been let out of the ground and were milling around the coach park.

"How the hell are we going to get in there?"

We didn't have much time to spare if we were to catch our flight from Manchester Airport so Whitby John went to ask one of the hundreds of coppers shadowing and protecting the visiting fans what we should do. Five minutes later we had a police escort.

None of us wear colours to matches so, at first, our 'friends' from Milton Keynes didn't realise who it was wandering among them. By the time they did, all 40 of us were on the coach.

The Scum fans had unfurled a banner reading 'MUFC – Istanbul Reds' during the game and thrown bars of Turkish Delight into the home seats – a clear reference to the murder of two Leeds fans the previous season. As our coach drove off, some of these oh-so-funny visiting fans started miming the actions of having their throats cut. And it is supposed to be us who are sick.

As we drive off down the M62, Whitby John asked the driver why he had parked there.

"I arrived about midday and the copper asked where I was going. I just said Manchester. I never thought anything else about it until all the away fans started coming out and you lot were nowhere to be seen."

"You'd think the copper would have known better. As if a coach returning to Manchester after the game would be for scum fans. They'll all be off back to Mummy and Daddy in Wales, Exeter or Millton Keynes now!"

I was looking forward to a few days away from home. My Dad's cancer was starting to hit him hard. Since Christmas, he had been in a lot of pain and unable to leave the house. I lived alone with my Dad so saw the pain he was going through. It was awful. A proud man, it was heart-breaking to see Dad reduced to someone who relied on those around him to get about. Due to the morphine he was taking to try to numb some of the pain, he was unable to drive. He was a season ticket-holder at Turf Moor, but hadn't been able to go to watch Burnley since a Boxing Day visit to Barnsley. That had hit him hard. Dad never complained, but in a way, that made it all the harder.

Dad wanted me to go to Madrid so went and stayed with my Gran for four days while I was away. I thought about Dad a lot on the flight to Madrid, but I was determined to have a good time. It was what he wanted.

On arrival in Madrid, we had to step across a mat of disinfectant to prevent us spreading foot-and-mouth around Spain. It wasn't the most foolproof way of preventing a possible spread though as it was only the shoes we were wearing that were disinfected and not those in our bags. A quick metro ride later and we arrived in the Gran Via area that housed our hotel. The scores of whores plying their trade on the street corner outside the hotel showed we were, once again, at the lower end of the price range.

We dumped our bags in the rooms and went out to enjoy a Saturday night in the Spanish capital. There weren't many other Leeds fans around so after enjoying a few bars, we decided to finish the evening in a nightclub.

"There's a big queue for this place, let's try in here," was Tally's verdict.

The doorman's reaction to five Englishman wanting to pay into the nightclub should have been a warning. "Are you sure, you want to come in here?"

"Yeah, why not? If it's shit we'll come straight back out."

So in we went. What we had failed to notice was that all the people in the queue outside were men, many of whom were sporting a Freddie Mercury-style moustache. It was a gay club. Unknown to us, we had spent the evening touring round the bars of the Spanish capital's version of Old Compton Street in London or the Gay Village in Manchester. We had a couple of drinks, but soon decided to call it a night. It had been a long day.

The usual suspects were on our trip, while Jay, a mate I have known since we were teenagers, was enjoying his first Euro away. Jay is a good mate, but a piss poor drinker. He doesn't go to away games that often, but if we've been out all day, you can guarantee he will fall asleep during the match. Leeds beat Chelsea 3-0 at Stamford Bridge in the mid-1990s, but Jay missed all three goals due to being asleep in his seat. Anyone wanting to nip out to the Gents or for something to eat at half-time had to step over Jay's slumped frame. He will also never live down a trip to Wimbledon a few years later when we bumped into Kevin Keegan on the train back north after the game. Keegan had just taken over at Fulham and with Kenny Dalglish having replaced him as Newcastle manager, Jay was obviously confused as he kept calling Keegan 'Kenny' all the way through our conversation. Keegan was too polite to correct him.

Leeds had been allocated 3,000 tickets for the Bernabeu and with most of us having been to all the European games, we had bought ours from Elland Road. Jay and Sean, a mate of Tally's from Doncaster, weren't so lucky so we decided to spend Sunday trying to buy a pair in the home end. I never enjoy watching Leeds while surrounded by opposition fans. I once sat through a 2-0 win at Chelsea on my own among the home fans and it was agony not being able to jump up and celebrate both goals. But if it is a choice between that and missing out then it has to be done. Jay and Sean's aim was to buy a ticket for the home end, but sneak into the Leeds seats with us. They need not have worried because Madrid sensibly sold tickets to the Leeds fans on the day before the game to ensure they could be segregated. In the end, an additional 5,000 United fans bought tickets in Spain to give the club its biggest support for a non-final tie in Europe.

We learned the ticket arrangements when visiting the Bernabeu on the Sunday morning. The club museum was open so we wandered in. It is an amazing sight with thousands of trophies and club memorabilia on show. We also had a wander out into the stadium and it is a truly breath-taking sight, comfortably better than Barcelona's Nou Camp. The obligatory photos were taken including a couple with the European Cup.

"We're practising for May the 23rd and the final," we told the club officials stood nearby, but they seemed to think we were joking.

The only downside to the tour was discovering that a Manchester United vase, handed over before the clubs met in a Champions League quarter-final, was on show. Jay subtly covered it up before we moved on. We ended the tour with a couple of drinks in the club bar and it was here that we met Steve McManaman.

The lanky Scouser had done well in Spain since leaving his hometown club Liverpool, and the Real fans mobbed him as he walked through the bar. We wandered over and had a chat about the previous night's 2-2 draw with Barcelona that Steve had played in. He seemed a decent, down-to-earth bloke who was just lucky enough to have the talent to earn £80,000 per week.

Despite the initial impression of Gran Via being of the whores working on the streets and the rather shady-looking pimps watching over them, our base was in fact ideal. Just a couple of minutes walk away was Puerta del Sol. Known to locals as merely Sol, it is as central as you can get in Madrid with a small plaque on the south side reading '0km' because distances along Spain's roads are measured from this point. It meant most areas were within walking distance of our hotel. I always prefer discovering a new city on foot

95

and Madrid did not disappoint. It may lack the beauty of Barcelona, but it certainly grows on you.

We fancied watching a bullfight, but were disappointed to find out none were planned during our visit. Instead, we contented ourselves with a relaxed walk around the city that included plenty of stop-offs in local bars.

By the day of the game, it was clear thousands of Leeds fans were in town. Locals told us that the previous season, Manchester United had brought 4,000 fans for their Champions League quarter-final, but we doubled that for a game which was meaningless due to both of us being already through.

Due to the huge number of Leeds fans inside the city, the policing was high profile. We arrived at an Irish bar in a side-street leading away from Sol and the atmosphere was relaxed. Several Leeds songs were given an airing and the mood was a happy one. It didn't last. Sean was the first to notice movement at the top of the alleyway leading to the Irish bar.

"Look at that lot. The riot police are moving into place and blocking off the alley."

The police pulling their visors down to cover their faces was our cue to get out of the way. Past experience has taught me that as soon as the visors are dropped, the police are ready to charge. We sneaked out of the alley round the back of the bar and continued having a few more relaxed drinks further away from Sol. By the time we returned an hour or so later, the Irish bar had been closed and there was broken glass littering the floor. What had happened, we weren't sure, but it didn't look too good. We popped into a bar nearby, but that was in the process of being closed as well.

We moved back into Sol and found a bar willing to stay open. Tension was now in the air, but it all seemed so unnecessary. Eventually, people started to drift towards the metro and the short ride to the Bernabeu and the atmosphere lightened. It was short-lived, however, and on arrival at Real Madrid's famous stadium, the tension had returned. The police were out in force at the turnstiles and indiscriminately hitting out at the Leeds fans who were only trying to get inside as kick-off approached.

A seven year old Leeds fan walked past holding his Dad's hand. Unfortunately, the young lad's flag inadvertently brushed against a policeman. Ignoring the fact it was an accident and the boy was so young, the copper turned round and attacked the Dad with his baton. It was disgusting, but as people started to argue with the police, they too felt the weight of a baton.

Graham has been a mate of Whitby John's for years. He's in his late 30s now, but we reckon he's still affected by something that happened when he was just eight. His Mum and Dad moved house in Whitby but forgot to tell Graham. So, at the end of his schoolday, Graham walked back to what was by now his old house and couldn't work out why no-one was there or why all the furniture had gone. A neighbour put him right and told him all the family had moved three miles away. Graham walked to his new house and was obviously a bit upset that his Mum and Dad had seemingly abandoned him. Graham arrived at his new house, but to make matters even worse, he then got a rocket off his Mum for missing his tea.

Due to the amount of times we have missed kick-offs, or even whole matches in Alec's case, Graham has stopped buying tickets for away matches. Instead, he will either spend the time we are at the stadium watching it on television or enjoying a few drinks in a quiet pub. His reasoning is that it saves him £25 to £30 a game. In Madrid, Graham was initially going to try to sneak in with us, but decided against it after the police had been so heavy-handed.

Instead, he opted for a bar directly outside the stadium where he could settle down and watch it on television. He had only been inside for a minute or so when a Real fan came running in off the street before knocking him to the ground with a cracking punch. By the time Graham got back up his attacker was long gone, but the bar owner was so ashamed by his countryman's actions that he gave this Englishman with a bloody nose free beer for the rest of the match.

The previous season, Manchester United fans had been breathalysed on the way into the stadium, but thankfully the police did not repeat it for our visit. If they had, we'd probably still have been in Madrid sobering up when Leeds played Lazio at Elland Road the following week.

By the time we took our seats on the back row of the top tier behind the goal, 15 minutes had elapsed and the score was already 1-1 with Alan Smith scoring for Leeds.

"Even setting off four days before a game is not early enough for us to make kick-off!"

As we had found out the previous Sunday during our stadium tour, the Bernabeu is impressive. Covered on three sides, the stands are steep and offer a great view of the action even when right at the back. We soon spotted Whitby John and the Doctor who, for some reason we couldn't fathom out, had wanted to spend the afternoon visiting a market. At half-time we also bumped into Pop and he told us about what has since become known as 'the hand of Sod', a re-working of Diego Maradona's equally suspect goal against England in 1986 when he claimed God had punched the ball into Peter Shilton's net.

Smithy had already put Leeds ahead when the ball came in from the left. Nigel Martyn looked set for a routine collection only for Raul to nip in and flick it into the net with his hand. Pop said it was obvious from the stands what had happened so how the referee and his two linesman missed it is a mystery. Who says cheats never prosper?

A lucky bounce gave Real a 2-1 lead at half-time when Luis Figo's cross hit a divot before flying over the helpless Leeds keeper. Half-time came and went with an energetic rendition of "We are the champions, the champions of Europe!", and once the game restarted, Leeds were soon level. Attacking our end, a cross came in from the left and Mark Viduka sent a bullet header past the keeper. I was glad because I had desperately wanted to see Leeds score in the Bernabeu. Raul then proved he is capable of playing by the rules by keeping his hands down while neatly flicking in a corner with his head.

Despite losing to a deflection and a hand-ball, the defeat was probably the least upsetting I have seen. The pressure was off with us already being through while we knew with a bit more luck we could have beaten Real Madrid on their own patch. There was certainly no disgrace in losing by the odd goal in five.

We were held in the Bernabeu for a few minutes and as we waited to leave, Tally spotted a familiar sight on the opposite side of the stadium.

"Isn't that Whitby John's flag near that exit?"

It was a fair distance away, but we soon spotted the Doctor's distinctive hair so knew it was the deadly duo. Whitby John said later that he wanted to wander round and take a photo of the away support.

"It was an amazing sight. To have 8,000 Leeds fans taking over one end of such a famous stadium was so impressive. No other club would have taken so many despite what the Geordies and Mancs say about them having the most loyal fans around."

The Spanish media the following day did not agree. In an amazing piece in a morning newspaper, the readers were treated to a piece with a headline of '8,000 hooligans have been in Madrid' and that 'Spain was glad to wave them goodbye'.

I had been in Madrid for four days and was stunned by the paper's verdict. We had seen the odd incident outside the turnstiles, but otherwise it had been trouble-free. After the fair account of our trip to Barcelona in the Spanish press, this was a shock. Thankfully, the papers after our subsequent trips to La Coruna and Valencia were full of praise for the Leeds fans, but the coverage after Madrid still rankles.

Despite the defeat, Leeds' run in Europe was set to continue and that left my mate Tony with mixed feelings. I have known Tony for years and we've enjoyed many cracking trips into Europe. He is not the luckiest of blokes though. Whether it be women, jobs or watching football – Tony always seems to be on the receiving end. He was arrested for flicking a 'V' sign at some Spurs fans in February, but for a variety of reasons, most not his fault, his case was not heard until after Euro 2000. By then the courts were cracking down hard on any football-related offence and where before he could have expected a fine for holding two fingers up, now he received a three year banning order. That meant every time Leeds play in Europe, he has to surrender his passport at the local police station. Leeds' best run in 26 years passed him by completely.

"I'm really pleased Leeds are doing well, but it is killing me not being able to go. Before this season, I had not missed a Euro away since 1992 so it is really hard. Every time I hand my passport in, I feel gutted."

It was difficult to know what to say when I spoke to him on the phone. He was missing out on a great season, but I didn't want to rub it in.

"If only my case had been heard before the summer, I'm sure it would have just been a fine. As soon as Euro 2000 happened, they started throwing three year bans around like confetti."

The abiding memory of Tony in Europe is of a trip to Monaco. It is not a cheap place to stay and he was running short of money so decided to break into a shop one evening. The Doctor and Tally knew what he was doing, told him he was stupid and walked away. Tony had only been gone a few minutes when they heard this almighty crash and a cry. Turned out he had tried to break into a shop through a skylight, but had instead crashed straight through it. He scarpered as quick as anyone can with a limp, and managed to get away before the police arrived.

Tony has been just as unlucky in love. For a night match with Newcastle a few years ago, he brought his then girlfriend to Elland Road and treated her to a day out as well as an overnight stay in Leeds. Unfortunately, the more she had to drink, the more amorous she became with all of us and eventually she sneaked off with Mick for a quick shag behind the Peacock pub. She eventually joined Tony inside Elland Road at half-time, claiming there had been a long queue outside. Tony even accepted her story until Mick told him the truth the following week.

Tony only managed one game before being banned and that was the 2-1 win over 1860 Munich back in August. He would again have to be content with watching Leeds' final group game, at home to Lazio, on ITV's highlights programme later that night. Even though the game was meaningless with Leeds guaranteed to finish second, Tony still wanted to be there. Unfortunately, he won't be allowed to set foot inside Elland Road until 2003 at the earliest.

Despite both sides resting key players, Tony missed an unexpectedly entertaining game. European nights are always pretty special at Elland Road, but I was not expecting too much from Lazio's visit. This fear seemed to be confirmed as I took my seat as the game kicked off with several players having been rested. Jacob Burns and Alan Maybury were both in the starting line-up for us, while Lazio gave several reserves a run-out. The pace initially mirrored what you would expect in a testimonial, but the antics of Fabrizio Ravanelli soon put an end to that.

I had always presumed that his 'The White Feather' nickname was something to do with his grey hair and not the fact that he is so easily blown over. If a Leeds defender came within five yards of Ravanelli, he was down quicker than you can say, "You cheating bastard!"

Ravanelli opened the scoring for Lazio only for Lee Bowyer to equalise with a lovely flighted shot that looped over the keeper and into the net. This prompted an amusing response from the Kop. It had recently been revealed that Lee Bowyer did not wear any underwear when he went out for the night and the response was swift.

"He's here, he's there,
He wears no underwear,
Lee Bowyer! Lee Bowyer!"

Our happy mood was short-lived though as Ravanelli was then shot by a sniper in the Kop – well, what other explanation can there be for the theatrics he produced when challenged by Dominic Matteo in the penalty area? Mihajlovic put Lazio back ahead from the spot, but justice was done just before half-time when Jason Wilcox equalised.

At half-time, talk turned to who we would be paired with in the quarter-final draw the following Friday. The sides I had wanted to avoid were Galatasaray, for obvious reasons, as well as Arsenal and Manchester United. I enjoy my trips into Europe so didn't fancy having to stay in England as opposed to being in Spain or Germany.

We would finish second regardless of the Lazio result that would see us paired with one of the sides who finished top of their group. That meant both Manchester United and Galatasaray were now out as they had finished second while Arsenal were also runners-up. We would now face Bayern Munich, Deportivo La Coruna or Valencia.

I had already been to Munich back in August, while La Coruna looked to be something of an outpost in northern Spain. Valencia was my preferred destination because the weather would be lovely and warm in mid-April. Whitby John wasn't fussed while the Doctor, who had spent much of half-time arguing with a steward who wouldn't let him into the bar because he didn't have his season ticket, fancied a return to Munich.

I was relieved we would not face Galatasaray in the quarter-finals, but there was still the possible nightmare scenario of meeting them in the Milan final. Such a prospect was just too dreadful to contemplate.

The Turks had quite clearly not cleaned up their act, as the riot 24 hours earlier in France during their 2-0 defeat against Paris St

Germain proved. They had ripped out seats and hurled them at riot police. 55 of the 56 fans arrested in the violence were Turkish. Despite this, UEFA's subsequent inquiry claimed the Turks played only a minor role in the trouble and were fined just £82,000. In contrast, Paris St Germain were hit with a £500,000 penalty while their ground was closed for three games. It seems the Turks are above the law.

UEFA took no action against Galatasaray after our visit in April, 2000, just as they hadn't after the visits by Manchester United and Chelsea in the 1990s. In fact, the only action taken after our UEFA Cup semi-final in Istanbul was to fine Leeds United because four of our players were booked. If awards had been handed out for bad taste then UEFA would have cleaned up over that.

In the immediate aftermath of the Paris violence – which caused the game to be held up for 20 minutes - UEFA claimed the trouble had been caused by Kurdish and Armenian opponents of Turkey. It began, according to the Turkish media, when an Armenian flag was unfurled to anger the fans of Galatasaray who, so charmingly, claim to live in a place called 'Hell'. They, of course, had to restore their national pride and four stewards were put in hospital in the trouble that followed. UEFA, amazingly, agreed with the claims of provocation.

After Heysel in 1985, there was no such mercy shown to English clubs as we were quite rightly banned from Europe. The horror of that night in Brussels was the culmination of a culture of violence that had surrounded English clubs for years. It had to be stopped and the ban worked. Turkish football seems incapable of putting its own house in order so, surely, UEFA should have acted after the Paris violence. A month later, UEFA finally seemed to have come to their senses as Galatasaray were banned from hosting European games at their cramped stadium due to safety fears. Unbelievably, this was soon overturned on appeal. I certainly didn't want Leeds facing Galatasaray again and I was mightily relieved to see the Turks knocked out by Real Madrid in the semi-finals.

Mark Viduka put Leeds ahead against Lazio in the second half and that looked like being enough only for Mihajlovic to equalise in the final minute. Lazio had apparently brought just six fans from Italy for the game and they looked suitably pleased with the draw as they celebrated near the back of the West Stand. My mind was already on the quarter-final draw and just who we would face. Getting this far was beyond anyone's wildest dreams, but now we were so close to a possible final it would be one hell of a blow to go out.

Chapter Nine

Are You Watching Manchester?

It was one of the best putdowns I've ever heard at Elland Road. Deportivo La Coruna had insulted us in the build-up to the first leg of our quarter-final tie, with midfielder Victor even going as far as describing us as "The weakest side left in the Champions League." He seemed to be suggesting we shouldn't even be in the last eight.

Unfortunately for Victor and his chums, this arrogance proved to be their downfall as Leeds destroyed Deportivo 3-0 with some of the best football I've seen at Elland Road. The chant began in the Kop about 15 minutes before the end with Leeds three goals ahead.

"3-0 to the weakest team!"

On and on it went as we taunted the Deportivo players, coaches and their small band of travelling fans. It was a wonderful moment and the fact the game was being shown live by ITV made it even sweeter. Manchester United had rather amusingly lost 1-0 at home to Bayern Munich the previous night in their quarter-final first leg so, again, it was difficult to resist the chance to have a dig at our rivals.

"Are you watching? Are you watching? Are you watching, Manchester?"

My mate Paul supports 'them' and he later told me how loud this came across on television. He had been pissed off with Bayern Munich's win anyway, but this just made him angrier.

Being drawn against Deportivo had initially left me with mixed feelings. Over the past year, I had been watching quite a bit of La Liga coverage on Sky Television and adopted Deportivo as 'my' team. Deportivo were either brilliant or awful, there was no middle ground. Just a few weeks earlier, Real Madrid had somehow escaped with a point from a televised 2-2 draw in La Coruna which should have finished at least 6-2 to the home side. The following week, however, Deportivo had lost 2-0 to a Las Palmas side that included the less than God-like footballer that is Vinny Samways. I was looking forward to visiting the Riazor Stadium, but was also worried Deportivo might knock us out.

The first leg took place at Elland Road and Leeds city centre was buzzing with anticipation throughout the afternoon. Everyone was talking about our first European Cup quarter-final in 26 years and whether Leeds could again rise to the occasion. In the Premiership, we were flying and had just won 2-0 at Sunderland. Compared to the previous season's win when the policing had been over the top, it had been a quiet trip to the North East.

In recent years, the policing at English grounds has improved dramatically. Hillsborough was a watershed for relations between fans and the police and the days of us being treated like animals are, in the main, long gone in this country. Any football fan who travelled in the 1980s will tell you the West Midlands force were the worst of the lot with random ejections and aggressive policing the norm at Villa, West Brom, Birmingham and Wolves. I once saw a lad thrown out at Villa Park for the crime of being 'sarcastic'. This approach always struck me as wrong because, in my experience, if you treat people badly then they will behave badly.

However, things have improved a lot since those dark days. I have even been called 'Sir' at Southampton and Coventry in recent seasons when being shown to my seat. However, at Sunderland in January, 2000, it seemed like we had stepped back in time. I arrived just before half-time with Tally due to our extended drinking session in Newcastle city centre earlier in the day and it was clear all was not right. Many Leeds fans, myself included, prefer to stand throughout games, but this did not go down well with the police. I lost count of the number of times that three coppers would march into the seats and order a couple of Leeds fans to sit down. I was warned myself before half-time, with one copper adding for good measure, "If you don't like it, we can discuss it downstairs if you like." I didn't fancy that as I knew I'd be ejected straight away.

At half-time, it got worse. I didn't arrive in the concourse until about five minutes into the break, but I walked into a full-scale battle between Leeds and the police. It certainly sobered me up.

I don't know how it started, but the riot police were soon brought in complete with visors and protective body armour. They forced

106

the Leeds fans into a corner, but that didn't stop several trying to charge back to regain ground. It went on for a good five minutes before, gradually, people started drifting back to their seats and calm was restored. Leeds won 2-1 and there were another couple of minor scuffles outside the Stadium of Light between Leeds and Sunderland fans.

We opted for a quick drink before catching the train to Newcastle, but apart from a few glares, we were left alone by the home fans who, to a man, were dressed in red and white stripes. I don't know what it is about the North East, but Sunderland and Newcastle fans seem to think wearing a football shirt is the height of fashion. Strange folk!

We had repeated our success at the Stadium of Light thanks to goals from Alan Smith and Mark Viduka to move up to third in the Premiership. The fact we had been 14th just three months earlier showed we were the form team. Deportivo would certainly be wary of us, no matter what their midfielder Victor said publicly.

We filed into Elland Road a couple of minutes before kick-off and took our seats in the Kop as a touching rendition of "Rocky, Rocky, Rocky Rocastle!" was sung in honour of our former midfielder. Just a couple of days earlier, Rocky had died from cancer at the tragically early age of just 33. We never saw the best of Rocastle during his time at Leeds, but he was still popular. My Dad's fight with cancer was entering its final stages and he had lost four stones in just three months. He had been in bed when I set off for the game and I have to admit the emotion nearly got the better of me as Rocastle's name was sung. Not for the first time, Leeds' European campaign managed to snap me out of any maudlin thoughts.

The first half went like a dream with Leeds, attacking the Kop, in electric form. We could have gone ahead as early as the second minute when the Deportivo keeper had to be at his best to save Lee Bowyer's shot. Ian Harte then went close with a bobbling shot that was smothered by the keeper, but we didn't have long to wait for the opening goal. And when it did arrive in the 25th minute it was a belter.

A free-kick 25 yards from the Kop goal is natural Ian Harte territory, and as he stepped up, I had a feeling the first goal was just seconds away. The Irishman had struggled for much of the season, but in the last month or so he had returned to form. Where before his free-kicks had been drifting harmlessly wide, now they were all hitting the target.

Harte duly ran towards the ball and swung his left foot at the ball to propel it over the wall and past the keeper. A perfect start.

"Ian Harte! Harte! Harte!"

The goal visibly lifted Leeds as shots rained in on the Deportivo goal. Even David Batty, hardly a regular scorer in his time at Leeds, tried his luck from 30 yards which prompted Whitby John, watching the replay on the Kop concourse at half-time, to say, "If Batty had scored that from 30 yards, I'd have booked my flight to Milan for the final tonight!"

Batty is loved at Elland Road. He keeps the side ticking in midfield and takes no shit from anyone. Anyone who doubts his influence at Elland Road since his return from Newcastle should look at the club's results when he has been in the side. In the 1999-2000 season we were riding high at the top of the League until Batty was injured, and our revival the following season also coincided with his return from injury after Christmas. He was running the game against Deportivo and more goals seemed certain in the second half.

Alan Smith made it 2-0 just after half-time before Rio Ferdinand's stooping header was enough to put us three goals in front. It was more than even the most optimistic of us could have dreamed of before kick-off. There were still 20 or so minutes left but if we could hold out then we were as good as through to the last four.

Victor was taunted for his pre-match comments about "the weakest team", but suddenly Deportivo came to life and the final minutes were a nightmare. A goal would have changed everything. But this was Leeds' night and Nigel Martyn ensured that the score remained at 3-0 when the final whistle blew. Just in case they hadn't got the message the first time, we treated our Manc friends at home to another rendition of "Are you watching, Manchester?" before strolling out into the night air as happy as I could recall all season. Everyone tried to talk at the same time.

"We're through. If we score once in Spain then they'll have to get five to go through. No chance!"

"I always fancy us to score away from home, no matter who we are playing."

Unbelievably, the Deportivo coach, Javier Irureta, couldn't even admit afterwards that his team had been well beaten. Laughably, he claimed, "If you sum up the goals, one was from a free-kick and the other two from corners. If you take those situations out of it we kind of matched them."

Er, yeah right. Whatever you say Mr Irureta! It was like claiming, "Well, if you take away the three Leeds goals then the game finished 0-0."

Nothing the Deportivo coach said could spoil our night and Leeds was a happy place with everyone apart from a handful of Spaniards grinning as if their Lottery numbers had come up.

Walking back through Holbeck after a game is something I often enjoy, but tonight was extra special. Everyone was laughing and smiling, with car drivers tooting their horns as they passed groups of Leeds fans. Some were warning that the job was only half done, but I wasn't listening. We were already in the semi-finals. I was right, but what I didn't know then was how close we would come to blowing it all.

Two weeks later we assembled at Stansted Airport. Tally was missing after losing his job a few weeks earlier, but otherwise it was the usual faces. La Coruna's location as an outpost on the north west coast of Spain meant we would not be flying direct. Or even to the same country. Whitby John initially tried to book flights to Lisbon in Portugal, but the game being played on Easter Tuesday meant the cost was far too high. Madrid was considered but while enjoying a few pre-match drinks before Leeds beat Charlton 2-1 at The Valley, we were told cheap flights were available to Biarritz in the south west of France. The same source also claimed La Coruna was a six hour car drive away or ten hours by train. It wasn't. But we didn't find that out until we had started driving across northern Spain. It was a hell of a lot more.

I travelled down to Stansted with Alec and Andy who, much to his disgust, had been saddled with the nickname 'Barthez' due to his likeness to the Manchester United keeper. He picked me up in Keighley at 5am and after putting his foot to the floor throughout the drive south, we pulled into the car park at Stansted just after eight. It might still have been early, but we headed straight for the bar to wait for Whitby John. We were now officially 'On Tour'.

John was travelling down from Whitby with Graham and 'Panface', so called by the Doctor because he "has a fucking flat face that looks like it's been smacked with a frying pan".

Panface is someone who ensures there is never a dull moment when we're away. He once bought a scooter and the first time anyone saw him driving it was when he was naked. He'd had a few one lunchtime and thought it'd be a great idea to drive round and round Whitby without anything on. Needless to say, his Lady Godiva impression is now legendary in the town.

The first bad piece of news came as I walked into the bar at Stansted with Alec and Barthez. My mobile phone rang and it was Whitby John.

"Graham is fucking useless."

"Er, right. Where are you?"

"We've only just set off from Whitby. The pillock was an hour late picking me up because he slept in. He turned up in a car with four bald tyres and one blew 50 yards down the road."

"But you are on the road now?"

"I haven't finished yet. We changed that tyre, but then another of the bald fuckers blew half an hour later. We had to wait for the breakdown van and have only just set off again. The stupid bastard."

I could hear Graham's voice in the background saying, "Calm down," but Whitby John just shouted, "Don't tell me to calm down you useless cunt."

I tried to divert his attention. "What time will you be getting here?"

"The plane flies at 11.40 and the gate closes half an hour before, but I don't think we'll make it. I'll ring when we get closer."

As we returned to our pints, we all agreed this was one car journey we were glad not to be part of. The atmosphere would be icy, to say the least.

Whitby John rang every half hour to update us on their progress and his mood, if anything, got worse.

"Can you go and ask the check-in if there is anywhere we can dump the car that is close to the terminal? The car park at Stansted is ten minutes away by bus and that could make all the difference."

I duly went and enquired, but the news was bad.

"You'll have to go to the normal car park and wait for the bus. And she said if you haven't checked in by ten past eleven at the latest then she won't let you on."

Whitby John swore at Graham for the umpteenth time that morning and told him to get his foot down. Thankfully, the still-not-speaking trio made it with just one minute to spare. The check-in desk said any later and they would definitely have had to wait until the following day because there is just one flight a day to Biarritz. Flying 24 hours later would not have left them with enough time to drive to La Coruna before the game kicked off. Whitby John has not missed a game for nearly 20 years so would not have been happy, but I think the most relieved man was Graham. Panface was just glad the drive was over because the silence in the car had been unbearable. Whitby John only started to calm down when the plane took off.

We regularly fly with budget airline Ryanair because they are cheap. It is a no-frills journey where you have to pay for any food and drink. Despite being in the Stansted bar for three hours before take-off and morning still not having turned into afternoon, I joined Barthez and Alec in a round of double vodka and cokes. At £18 a go, they weren't cheap but we got stuck in anyway. Six rounds later and we more or less fell off the plane in France.

Before leaving England, I had been designated as the map reader in the first of the two cars that we hired to travel from Biarritz to La Coruna. It was my job to stay awake and direct us through northern Spain. I protested that my map-reading may be hampered by how much I'd drunk, but I was told, "You'll be fine."

I clambered into the passenger seat of our 'People Carrier' alongside Graham, and managed to find Spain – sounds quite easy, but you'd be surprised! Our first problem came at the border when we had to pay a road toll. Graham, who had spent 20 minutes of the flight giving Whitby John the benefit of his advice about how to drive abroad, pulled our 'People Carrier' up to the booth only to find he had chosen a closed one. He started to reverse, but didn't realise Whitby John had followed him in the car behind. Two seconds later and we hit the second hire car. Thankfully, there wasn't much damage so we set off again.

After finding Spain I also managed to ensure we were on the correct road to take us along the coast and past Bilbao, Santander

111

and Oviedo before completing the final leg to La Coruna. That was the planned route anyway.

Unfortunately, the vodka and lager had started to kick in as we passed Bilbao and instead of directing us past Santander, I sent us straight into the city centre. I looked forlornly for a sign, but none appeared. The mobile suddenly rang and it was Whitby John. He was still on a short fuse after the drive to Stansted.

"Where the fuck are we? Have you got us lost already?"

"No, not at all," I lied. "I've just looked at the map and it will all come right once we get round this corner."

Five seconds later and everyone in the 'People Carrier' collapsed into laughter as we arrived at a dead-end with a lighthouse looking out across the coast. John obviously wasn't amused as he started shouting and bawling. I promptly resigned as map-reader and let some other poor sod take over.

We soon realised La Coruna was a lot further from Biarritz than we had been led to believe. This, coupled with the mind-numbingly boring roads in northern Spain, meant I soon started to lose the will to live. If it hadn't been for the Doctor, I think we'd all have fallen asleep. Every time we overtook the car containing Whitby John, Barthez, Panface and Alec, he would say, "My God! That is one fucking ugly car. Those four are so ugly, that car should only be allowed out at night!"

We must have passed each other ten times every hour and the Doctor marked every one with the same phrase. I don't know whether it was the hysteria of being cooped up in the car so long, but at the time it was the funniest thing any of us had ever heard.

After travelling for eight hours we decided to stop at a town called Leon - still 180 miles short of La Coruna, but none of us could handle travelling any further. While looking for a hotel, Graham twice drove the wrong way up a one-way street that didn't please the drivers coming the other way. A quick shout of "Inglese!" while reversing back down the street, this time avoiding John, sorted us out both times.

Eventually we parked up, found a decent hotel and went out hunting for a good time. Unfortunately, the best we could find was a karaoke bar that we managed to clear with a rather tuneless rendition of *Let It Be*. Butchering is too kind a word for what we did to The Beatles' classic. After spending so long driving in hot conditions, the beer was initially flying down our throats, but tiredness soon crept in and we called it a night.

The morning of matchday began with all eleven of us nursing hangovers, but we were on the road very quickly. The Doctor continued to abuse the 'Ugly Truck' all the way to La Coruna and we eventually arrived in Sada, a town just a couple of miles away, in the middle of the afternoon. Our arrival was not as smooth as we had been hoping though.

Graham had driven all the way from Biarritz and was distinctly fed up as we, lost again, vainly searched for a sign directing us to Sada. If we went the wrong way, he would simply drag the 'People Carrier' through a U-turn regardless of any cars around us. He did this twice on a double carriageway in the centre of La Coruna with a motorcyclist having a lucky escape as we pulled straight across him. A car driver who Graham later cut up also shouted abuse at us, but he was soon quietened as the Doctor jumped out and chased after him while shouting "Come here you foreign bastard!"

The local took the sensible option and sped off as this rather strange looking Englishman ran towards his car. We dumped our bags in the hotel and caught the bus to La Coruna. After a couple of leisurely drinks in bars near the city centre, we caught a taxi to the harbour that houses Deportivo's Riazor Stadium.

Located on the sea-front, it certainly has the best location of any football ground I have been to. It was windy, but with the sun beating down, it was a step up from traipsing through the back streets of Moss Side or Tottenham ahead of a game.

We opted for a drink in the supporters' club, situated on the beach just a short stroll from the stadium. The local newspaper caused a few laughs with the injured trio of Michael Duberry, Stephen McPhail and Michael Bridges all in our alleged starting line-up along with Matthew Jones, who had signed for Leicester four months earlier. Danny Mills also looked to be in for a busy night because he was listed as playing at right back and centre forward. I was also surprised to learn we had lost the 1977 European Cup final to Liverpool. We moved to another couple of bars along the sea-front and the Doctor decided to give his party piece an airing.

For reasons that I'll never understand, the Doctor is obsessed with getting his cock out in front of a crowd. He's very proud of it. I've lost count of the number of times it is whipped out and placed in some unsuspecting lad's back-pocket. As you'd expect, it makes them jump.

One of the Doctor's favourite tricks is to walk up to a stranger and ask, "Do you want a cock fight, mate? You can have two strikes to my one."

Usually, a look of horror will spread across a victim's face while he stammers "Er . . . n-no."

In La Coruna, the Doctor started his usual routine on a Leeds fan who was so pissed I doubt he even knew which city he was in. We were expecting the usual response.

"A cock fight? What's one of them?"

"You can have two cracks on my cock to my one and the bout goes on until one man concedes."

"Yeah. All right then. I'll have a go."

I looked at Whitby John and laughed. The Doctor had found an opponent.

Graham was the first to speak. "I hope he gets about 12 inches out and batters the Doctor. It'll stop him doing it again."

Unfortunately for us, the Doctor's opponent whipped out a tiddler and the bout was soon over amid huge roars of laughter from our corner of the bar. The Doctor was certainly pleased with his victory. Whitby John, for reasons known only to himself, took a photo of the 'bout' which must have raised a few eyebrows in Boots when the film was developed.

The home fans were certainly confident of victory. Everywhere we went, they would either say "4-0!" or put up four fingers. They were very friendly and their confidence was a bit unnerving, but I still felt Leeds would go through. As kick-off approached, we decided to make a move. I started to walk back towards the Riazor with Whitby John and the Doctor while Barthez, Graham and Panface said they would follow on after finishing their drinks.

A couple of minutes later and we were stood outside the stadium when the turnstiles were suddenly closed. The police were trying to usher us away. "The Leeds seats are full. No more of you will be allowed into the stadium."

We were stood in a group of around 100 Leeds and were not happy. "We've come all this way and have got tickets. Let us in you tossers!"

The police would not be moved though. In their wisdom, they had rounded up around 300 Leeds fans that had bought tickets for the home end and escorted them into the away enclosure. That meant it was now full. This wasn't our fault though. We'd travelled a long way, spent a lot of money and had tickets to watch the game in our pockets.

Inevitably, there was some pushing and shoving and the police's response to this was to charge at us on horseback. I have never been too keen on police horses since I saw one kick out wildly while we were being escorted away from Leicester City's Filbert Street in the late 1980s. A Leeds fan had nipped the horse on the arse - not the most sensible thing I've ever seen! - and since then I have kept well away from them.

After a couple of hairy moments outside Deportivo's stadium that saw us pushed around by the horses, the police finally opted for common sense and let us in. They hadn't finished though. Once through the turnstiles, I was attacked from both sides. I wasn't the only one either with several fans being indiscriminately hit with batons. I put my arms up to try to protect myself as I pushed at the line of police. One lad had blood pouring from his head, but as his mate protested, both were clubbed to the floor. The four-legged animals outside were nothing compared to these animals inside the stadium. It was all so unnecessary. Why the police had been so aggressive was a mystery, but no doubt if the incident had reached the press then it would have been automatically assumed it was 'Leeds fans playing up again'.

The atmosphere was fraught with around 50 fired-up Englishmen stood around arguing with the police before a couple of Leeds fans calmed the situation down. The game was 15 minutes old when we arrived in the seats and Leeds were already 1-0 down. Just the start we didn't need.

The early goal meant the atmosphere inside the Riazor had been cranked up. Deportivo looked confident of repeating their feat earlier in the season when they beat Paris St Germain 4-3 after being three goals behind. This was going to be a long night.

Moving so many fans from the home seats also meant the away enclosure was uncomfortably packed. The lessons of Hillsborough obviously hadn't reached northern Spain. After arriving so late, the only vantage point we could find was near the main entrance to the seats. I spent the first half perched on the edge of a step and the slightest movement from the crowd following the game meant I was pushed over the edge and on to the seats in front. It was chaos.

I missed Alan Smith going round the keeper and shooting into the side-netting because I was on the floor after a surge. The area being all-seater just made it worse because the seats caused people to trip and fall to the floor far more often than would have been the case on a terrace.

Making English stadiums all-seater is something I have never agreed with. It was not the terraces that were to blame for Hillsborough. It was the management of the Leppings Lane terrace on the 15th of April, 1989, that caused 96 people to suffocate in the Sheffield open air. I would love to see a return to terracing, but as long as the clubs and police say otherwise, it isn't going to happen. I am not talking about the huge 20,000-plus capacity terraces of the past. The days of the Anfield Kop or South Bank at Molineux are long gone.

Instead, English football should follow the example of Germany where several stadiums have small areas that can be converted from standing to seats when the need arises such as a European tie. Such a move would also eradicate the frequent problem at Elland Road of everyone on the Kop having to stand for 90 minutes when some would rather sit. I also prefer standing. But despite a sizeable majority of fans welcoming a return to terracing, it won't happen until the opinion of the Government and football authorities change.

Leeds had been rattled to go behind so early on and the swagger of our European campaign disappeared as the ball was given away carelessly. Harry Kewell was the first to feel the force of the Leeds' fans anger as he failed to track back after losing the ball.

"Move you lazy Australian bastard! Why don't you fuck off if you can't be bothered getting stuck in!"

I felt the criticism harsh bearing in mind what Harry brings to the Leeds side, but with nerves fraying on and off the pitch, it was perhaps understandable.

Just a few days earlier, Leeds had produced a brilliant display to win 2-1 at Liverpool. The first 45 minutes at Anfield had been our best of the season so it was a mystery why we were playing so badly in Spain. Rio Ferdinand cleared off the line while Nigel Martyn

116

had to be at his best to prevent us falling further behind. It was such a mess that Lee Bowyer and Mark Viduka started arguing out on the field – always a very bad sign for a team.

The half-time whistle was met with relief. We wandered back downstairs as another tense stand off between the police and Leeds fans developed. The local force certainly seemed ready for action as they tapped their batons into their gloved palms, waiting for the signal to crack some English heads again. The tension was again defused, with the Leeds' police who travel abroad stepping in to calm the situation.

Back out on the pitch, it wasn't quite so easy to defuse Deportivo's attack as they chased the vital second goal while we looked like the occasion had got to us.

Victor, whose pre-first leg assessment of Leeds now looked spot on, looked like he had scored, only for Ian Harte to clear from under his own crossbar. Nigel Martyn then saved a close-range shot and I asked Whitby John how long to go.

"Half an hour to go yet."

30 minutes! I felt there was no way we would hold on. Deportivo were in control and I felt they had to score again soon. A second goal was inevitable and a quickly taken free-kick let Tristan in and we were now just 3-2 ahead on aggregate. I again asked Whitby John how long to go.

"17 minutes."

I wasn't the only one thinking we had blown it. But then, we had hope. At the far end of the stadium and with the Deportivo defence too far upfield, Olivier Dacourt found Mark Viduka with a fine pass. This looked like the moment we had been waiting for.

I held my breath. Surely, this was the goal that would put us through. Viduka steadied himself and then drilled a low shot to the left of keeper Francisco Molina. It looked a goal all the way only for Molina to dive low and somehow block the ball with his arm. The groans around me told their own story. We had missed a great chance and another goal now would surely be the end.

Amazingly, the late Deportivo onslaught I feared never materialised and after what felt like an age, the final whistle was blown. It was the sweetest sound imaginable. I hugged Whitby John and the Doctor, more in relief than celebration. At last, our

117

ordeal was over. The mind-numbingly boring journey across northern Spain was suddenly worth it. Even the thought of the return trip the following day couldn't spoil the moment.

Unlike Milan or Anderlecht, the celebrations were more of relief than anything else. We were through, but we had come mighty close to blowing it. If Deportivo had equalised, I am in no doubt that we would have lost in extra-time. The players returned to the field five minutes after the final whistle and came across to return our applause.

A group of Deportivo fans in front of us unveiled a Turkish flag, which, at the time, we felt was a sick reference to the two Leeds fans killed in Istanbul a year earlier. I later discovered that a fanatical group of home fans have called themselves The Turk Boys for years and this flag is flown at every Deportivo game. After about 20 minutes of being held in the stadium by the police, we were allowed to file out of the Riazor and headed for the Deportivo supporters club. Again, the feeling among all the Leeds fans inside was one of relief rather than celebration. I felt like I'd aged ten years during the past two hours.

A quick phone call to England revealed Valencia would be our opponents in the semi-finals. The semi-finals? It was only when Whitby John said those magical words that it registered that we were in the last four! All season I had been expecting us to be knocked out and yet, here we were, planning a return to Spain for a semi-final second leg in three weeks time. We were the only English representatives left in the European Cup and that made the moment even sweeter.

I joined Whitby John and the Doctor in walking back along the sea-front before nipping into Limericks Irish Bar for a celebratory few drinks. We were only half-way through our first beer when the police came charging into the pub and pulled a Leeds fan outside. He was immediately followed by three Deportivo fans who managed to calm the police down and explain what had happened.

"He did not cause the fighting. He was provoked by one of our fans who pushed him over for no reason. You should arrest the Deportivo fan instead."

This was an unexpected development for the two officers holding the Leeds fan and they seemed unsure what to do next. Thankfully, his superior ordered the release of the Leeds fan before they escorted the Spaniard away from Limericks. The 'reprieved' Leeds fan bought his three new friends a drink as a thank you for helping him out.

We sat talking to a group of local fans for about an hour and they were the friendliest we had met all season. To a man, they all now wanted us to go on and win the Champions League. I doubted I would have been so gracious in defeat. We passed a pleasant hour talking to the locals outside Limericks before going looking for a livelier venue. It was then that we bumped into Alec, Graham, Panface and Barthez. They were all legless.

We hadn't seen them inside the stadium so asked them where they had been sat.

"Oh, we never went. We were sat in that bar you left us in when the game kicked off. It was on television and we were so comfortable that we couldn't be bothered moving."

"You mean you didn't go in at all?"

"Nope. We thought about leaving but at that moment, the barman asked us what we wanted to drink so we decided to stay."

I had to laugh. Il four of them had travelled more than 1,000 miles, most of these by road, they all had match tickets,and the trip would cost them around £500 each. Despite this, they opted to sit in a bar just 50 yards from the stadium and watch the game on television. God knows what a psychiatrist would make of this behaviour!

The night passed in an alcoholic haze and finished in the only place still serving beer at six in the morning, a brothel. The girls had all finished working for the night, but the owner welcomed the chance to earn a few extra pesetas by selling us some over-priced, warm beer. We weren't complaining though. We were through to the semi-finals and I for one didn't want the night to end.

Waking up with another hangover the following morning, the prospect of a 600 mile drive back to the airport at Biarritz didn't exactly fill us with excitement so we decided to aim for Santander. We would then complete the trip to France on Thursday morning. We opted for a different return route – I was still suspended from map-reading duties – and found Santander with no difficulties. It took nine hours and apart from the spectacular scenery around Oviedo, it was a pretty dull trip with only the Doctor's routine "That is an ugly car . . . " comments keeping spirits up. The four occupants of the 'ugly car' weren't too happy with their new tag so decided to call us, with a heavy hint of irony, the 'male models car'.

One upsetting sight during the trip was a dog being run over by a huge lorry that left the poor animal thrashing around in pain. We were four cars behind the lorry and I felt sick as the dog, with the back half of its body flattened, being dragged away by its owner to be put out of its misery. Even the Doctor was quiet for the next half hour or so. It wasn't long before he piped up again though and as we sat down for a meal in a service station, he said, "I'll have the dog please!" to the non-plussed waitress.

Santander was another excellent choice for a night out. Manchester United and Galatasaray both crashed out of the Champions League live on television so a few celebratory drinks were in order. We called it a night at about three the following morning but Macca, Wayne and Paul, who had travelled with us in the People Carrier, decided to carry on drinking. It was agreed we would meet up at 10am before completing our journey to Biarritz.

After a decent night's sleep, food was uppermost in my mind as I joined Alec in a hunt for breakfast. As we came out of the hotel we heard the familiar sound of *Marching On Together* approaching round the corner and wondered who it could be. We soon got our answer as Macca, Wayne and Paul came stumbling round the corner. They were paralytic and hadn't been back to the hotel all night.

It was 15 minutes before we were due to set off so all three trooped up to the room, collected their bags and went to the hotel bar and ordered three beers. Needless to say, we had only been driving for half an hour when Macca and Paul fell asleep. Wayne stayed awake for another ten minutes, but then even he had to give up and grab some much needed sleep. All three are the sort of lads that are great to travel away to watch Leeds with. They love a beer and a laugh and boast a huge number of stories.

My favourite involves Wayne and a dispute he had with a neighbour who complained about anything and everything. One day, Wayne had had enough and walked round, picked the neighbour up and carried him back round to his own house. Wayne then opened a grate on his drive and shoved the neighbour in it before replacing the lid. Wayne walked calmly back into his house, put the television on and forgot all about his trapped neighbour.

His wife had been home ten minutes when she asked what that strange noise was, as though someone's shout for attention was being muffled. Wayne suddenly remembered the neighbour and went and let him out. Needless to say, the rather shaken neighbour didn't complain about anything again and within a couple of weeks had moved away. One of the more 'interesting' ways to resolve neighbourly disputes!

Our far from sleeping beauties woke up just a few miles short of Biarritz and the conversation turned to how we were going to get to Valencia. Paul thought this was a good opportunity to phone his wife.

"Hiya, love. I'm just ringing to see how you are. Has everything been okay?"

He continued in this vein for a couple of minutes before casually tossing in, "I'm thinking of going to Valencia for the second week in May."

We could tell his wife wasn't happy by the look on his face. We were trying not to laugh in the background as Paul mumbled, "Don't be like that, love."

He came off the phone looking crest-fallen.

Graham was the first to speak. "Your lass all right, is she?"

"Not really. She's just given me a right mouthful. I think her exact words were, 'You phone me up for the first time in three days to tell me you are going to Valencia. Well, you can piss off.' I tried to calm her down, but you lot laughing in the background didn't help. Her final words were, 'And you can tell your mates they're all knobheads as well'."

Despite the verbal lashing he'd had, Paul was adamant.

"I'm definitely going though. I think I might need to stay at yours tonight, Wayne, but she's not stopping me going to the semi. No doubt my gear will be in matching bin bags on the lawn when I get home."

As Graham pulled into the car park at Biarritz airport, we all agreed that never again would we travel so far by road. A 1,200 mile round trip by road is too far and meant we had spent the best part of three days in the car. There were plus points though. It had been another classic trip. We had managed three nights in three different cities, something I prefer to staying in one place for the whole trip. We had also enjoyed many, many laughs. They weren't over either. Alec had been asleep in the back of Whitby John's car all the way back to France and was still half-asleep as we boarded the plane.

As the steward brought the duty frees round halfway through the flight, Alec piped up. "I've only got pesetas because we haven't spent any time in France. Can I use them to buy some perfume for my girlfriend?"

"We take pesetas, francs and sterling, sir."

Alec obviously mis-heard the steward and his bottom lip came out. "I won't have anything then. I've only got pesetas. Bollocks to you!"

The six rows either side of Alec fell about laughing as he went into a huff at not being able to use his Spanish currency. We were all tired after three days on the road, but Alec had, yet again, inadvertently lifted our spirits. Roll on Valencia.

Chapter Ten

So Near . . .

Sharing a birthday with David Beckham is not something I am proud of. I am sure the Manchester United midfielder is a thoroughly nice bloke who, we are reliably informed by a sycophantic media, is a great husband and father. Bully for him. I also admit he is one of the best footballers England has produced in the past 20 years. But the fact is I don't like 'Becks', as the media annoyingly refer to him assuming he is the nation's mate. I admit it is a completely irrational dislike because I have never met him.

But if Beckham is on the front of a newspaper, I won't buy it. I'm just not interested in what his new house looks like or how many cars he owns. It may be jealousy or it may be because he plays for a football club that I don't like. I'm not sure. But whatever it is, I'm not a fan. And that means my mates take great pleasure in winding me up on the 2nd of May every year as 'we' celebrate our shared birthday. David O'Leary was also born on the same day, but they choose to ignore this.

Being born in the first week of May means I have often celebrated my birthday watching Leeds United. My 19th birthday was very special because Leeds collected the League title at Elland Road before going on to beat Norwich 1-0. We had clinched the Championship the previous week thanks to a 3-2 win at Sheffield United and Manchester United's defeat at Liverpool. Living in London at the time meant a week of celebrations in the capital among Chelsea, West Ham, Arsenal and Manchester United fans before travelling north to watch Rodney Wallace's solo goal beat Norwich. It was a birthday that will be hard to better.

There have been other Leeds games on my birthday with a 1-0 home win over Crystal Palace in 1988 standing out. The football was pretty unremarkable, but the scenes after the game when thousands of us refused to leave for nearly an hour after our final home game as we chanted for the team illustrated just how loyal, or desperate, Leeds fans had become. We finished seventh in Division Two that season, well adrift of the play-offs.

My 28th birthday, however, promised something equally as memorable as that remarkable day when my team were presented with the Championship back in 1992. Leeds were facing Valencia in a European Cup semi-final first leg at Elland Road. If we could somehow repeat the three goal victory of the quarter-finals then, I decided, it would be my happiest birthday ever. David O'Leary obviously felt the same, saying the present he really wanted for his 43rd birthday was a commanding first leg lead.

To help celebrate my birthday, Jay and Drew had both booked the day off work so we started drinking early in Bradford before moving on to Leeds midway through the afternoon. We met a few mates during their lunch hour in Bradford and with it being my birthday, pint after pint of Stella was thrust into my hand.

It turned into a session and a half and I managed to lose an hour or so late in the afternoon. A couple of days later, I bumped into someone I used to go to school with and started chatting. It turned out I had been talking to him for about 20 minutes outside the Wetherspoon's pub in Leeds Station before the Valencia game. I couldn't even remember seeing him, never mind what we were talking about.

We eventually set off by taxi for The Britannia in Holbeck to meet Tally for one last drink before the ten minute walk to Elland Road. The game had sold out within hours of the tickets going on sale as we stood just 180 minutes away from the European Cup final. It all felt slightly surreal as we crossed the footbridge over the M621 with Elland Road straight ahead of us. I've made this walk hundreds of times in the past, but this was different.

During the 1980s when I first started watching Leeds, sell-outs were almost unheard of. A quick glance at the record books tells me the Crystal Palace game on my birthday in 1988 was watched by a crowd of 13,217. That was by no means the lowest during our eight year spell in the Second Division with Carlisle's visit to Elland Road in May 1984 seeing just 8,278 watching a 3-0 home win. Crowds improved as the decade went on, but before the promotion season of 1989-90, an attendance of more than 20,000 was a notable achievement.

I can only recall two games where it was a scramble to ensure I was inside before the turnstiles were slammed shut. These were an FA Cup fifth round tie with QPR in 1987 and a New Year's Day derby clash with Bradford City the following season. We won both games, but it was the panic that set in as we pushed and shoved our way into Elland Road that I will never forget. The QPR game, in particular, saw gate after gate closed with me still outside and kick-off still more than an hour away.

This was pre-Hillsborough and the queues outside the back of the Kop were chaotic with just a seething mass of people trying to get in. I didn't fancy fighting my way through that so I paid to get into the Lowfields side of the ground. I was still only 14 and had always watched Leeds from the back of the Kop, left side. The Lowfields, and particularly the aptly named 'Looney Pen' that was situated next to the away fans, was where the older lads would stand. Along with everyone else on the Kop, I would offer encouragement with chants of "Lowfields, Lowfields, do your job!" as the away fans stood nervously awaiting a possible invasion.

Whether the Leeds 'boys' really needed the encouragement of this particular teenage fan is debatable, but I felt like I was doing my bit! I only went in the Lowfields on one other occasion and that was for a game with Chelsea in 1988. I was 15 by now so decided the small terrace was the place to be for our biggest game of the season. In those days, I felt Manchester United were not true rivals because we never played them.

The Lowfields terrace was packed a long time before kick-off and, in truth, I could hardly see the pitch as we lost 2-0. But what I'll never forget from that afternoon was the hatred that poured out from those around me towards the away fans in the South Stand. After the game, the Leeds fans, frustrated at not being able to attack their Chelsea counterparts, smashed up a car showroom on the walk back to the city centre.

Matchday at Elland Road today is very different to the 1980s. As I passed through the Kop turnstiles, no disorderly queues this time. I knew the atmosphere would be highly charged but nothing like that afternoon against Chelsea, which I have to admit I'd enjoyed, 13 years earlier.

Leeds started well and should have been ahead at the break. Ian Harte's deep cross was headed back across goal by Harry Kewell.

Rio Ferdinand then flicked on the ball and Mark Viduka looked ideally placed to put the ball into the net only for Alan Smith to jump and flick the ball wide. Like thousands of us inside Elland Road, Smithy held his head as the crucial chance went begging.

Lee Bowyer went even closer when Smithy's shot was deflected off a Valencia defender and towards the Leeds midfielder. He nodded the ball towards goal and I really thought it was going in and started celebrating. Unfortunately, the ball crashed against the crossbar and we were denied once again. The breakthrough just wouldn't come.

My heart was in my mouth in the final seconds, however, when a Vicente volley bounced up and over Nigel Martyn and towards the top corner. Rio Ferdinand somehow got back and flicked the ball to safety from under the crossbar. What a reprieve. There was a great photo in the national newspapers the following day of Rio nodding the ball clear. As if to illustrate the collective spirit which exists at Leeds, David Batty is also straining every inch of his 5 foot 8 inch frame just behind Ferdinand in a bid to ensure the ball does not cross the line.

It had been a semi-final of cat and mouse with neither side dominating the game. Valencia were happier with the goalless draw, but at least, we thought, the Spanish side didn't have a crucial away goal. If we could score in the Mestella then they would have to score twice.

Prior to the game, Valencia coach Hector Cuper had instructed his side to practice tugging shirts and tackling from behind so they would be ready to match Leeds' alleged physical approach. The Spanish media were also predicting a bloodbath at Elland Road, but it had never materialised. There had been a minor skirmish involving Lee Bowyer, but from the Kop it had not looked serious. Unfortunately, UEFA did not agree and the following Monday our hopes of reaching the final would be badly hit by Bowyer's subsequent suspension.

We knew none of this though as we set off for southern Spain. With temperatures up in the 80s and Valencia being close to Benidorm, it was clear God must be a Leeds United fan. The heat was stifling the moment we arrived in Spain and a pleasant change from the dull skies we had left behind in Yorkshire.

The previous weekend I had been at Arsenal when a 2-1 defeat meant Liverpool were now odds-on to finish third and qualify for next season's Champions League. It had still been an enjoyable afternoon though with Martin Keown coming in for some almighty stick from the Leeds fans. Hardly in the David Beckham league when it comes to looks, the Gunners defender was serenaded with an incessant chant of "Keown is an ugly cunt, Keown is an ugly cunt!"

Unsurprisingly, he didn't seem too impressed although I noticed several of Keown's team-mates laughing at his expense. We also taunted the home fans over their quarter-final exit from the Champions League with chants of "What you doing Tuesday night?"

"Going out on Tuesday night!" was their impressively swift retort, but it was clear we had touched a raw nerve.

The defeat on the pitch, however, meant that if we were to again take part in the Champions League, we would have to win the Milan final on the 23rd of May. Before that though, we had the small matter of last season's finalists Valencia in their stadium standing between us and a tilt at glory.

Travelling abroad to watch the team is something every Leeds fan should try. Three or four days away with your mates having a drink and a laugh is enjoyable enough, but if Leeds manage to win on European soil then it is money well spent. Sometimes, though, things don't quite go to plan.

Whitby John once went on a pre-season tour of Malaysia and it was an experience he'll never forget. He was in a group of around ten Leeds fans who had enjoyed a few drinks and were treating the locals in a bar to a trip through the United back catalogue of songs. Eventually, however, the barman called time. Whitby John and the rest never heard him so the singing continued. All of a sudden, the barman rushed out from behind the counter brandishing a samurai sword. It was a much more effective way of clearing the bar than "Time Gentlemen, please," and Whitby John and the rest of the lads took the hint. Unfortunately, on their way out, one turned round to apologise for the singing, but the barman just swung the sword at him. He pulled away sharpish, but still received a cut to his hand. It could have been a lot worse.

Later in the same trip, Whitby John had started chatting to an English lad who lived locally. He turned out to be a Manchester

United fan who started getting agitated by his team having the piss ripped out of it relentlessly.

Eventually he snapped. "One phone call and I can have 20 lads down here and they'll kill you. They have guns."

With perfect timing, Whitby John and the rest of the Leeds fans replied in unison. "You'll have to reach the phone first, pal."

The Manc took the hint and left the bar. Bearing in mind what had happened with the samurai swordsman a day earlier, the Leeds lads also decided it was time to leave just in case this exiled Manc did return with a gun.

Valencia was a much calmer place than Malaysia. Many Leeds fans plumped for a few days in Alicante and the surrounding Costa Blanca resorts that were packed with holidaymakers. While Valencia was relatively quiet on the eve of the second leg, Alicante was bouncing. Whitby John, Tally, Alec, Barthez and the usual suspects arrived early evening.

Alec had obviously not learnt from the flight to Biarritz before the Deportivo game because he again got stuck into the drink. On arrival at the hotel, he was plastered and sat down at the bar. Within a minute he was fast asleep. He couldn't be woken so the rest of the lads left him there when they went out for the night. Amazingly, on their return eight hours later, the bar was closed, but Alec was still sat there, slumped forward with his bag next to him. Whitby John finally managed to wake Alec before helping him up the steps to bed where he slept for another ten hours.

The morning of the game and the city's beaches were the place to be. Leeds flags were hoisted on every available fence or wall while we soaked up the sun, beer and party atmosphere that had developed. It was a wonderful place to be with impromptu games of football taking place and music booming out across the area. The following day's Spanish press spoke, again in a surprised tone, of the party atmosphere that surrounded the travelling fans on the beach. Maybe one day the misconception of all English football fans being a motley crew of savages, rapists and trained killers will change but I'm not holding my breath.

Valencia is a fine city with a very pleasant Old Town area to wander round. The city is split by the Rio Turia, a once mighty river which is now dry and being turned into a city-length park, the Jardines del Turia. Again, this was an enjoyable place to while away an hour or so. As pleasant as it was passing the day either in the town or on the beach, no-one could forget just why we were here. Leeds were just 90 minutes from the final. I was getting more and more nervous as kick-off grew closer.

Arriving in the Plaza Del Valencia CF behind the main stand at the Mestella about an hour or so before kick-off, it was clear tension was in the air. Groups of Leeds and Valencia fans were mingling with just a sprinkling of police officers stood around idly. At first, it was just a few verbal insults being swapped between individual fans but trouble looked inevitable.

The first hail of missiles came from a bar on the far corner of the square from the stadium. Bottles and plastic garden chairs, seemingly now de rigueur for any hooligan-to-be, were thrown as the police charged in to try to restore order. The Leeds fans, heavily outnumbered by now, were shepherded into a bar in the far corner of the square. The Valencia fans gradually started moving across the square and it wasn't long before the bottles started flying again. Most tried to take cover although one Leeds fan, obviously the worse for wear, decided to either catch the bottles or try to kick them away. Needless to say this led to him being covered in blood seconds later. The police, true to form, charged at the English fans and started to usher us away from the area and round to the away seat turnstiles. Kick-off was now just 20 minutes away so there weren't too many objections.

The main talking point during the day had been the extraordinarily late suspension of Lee Bowyer. UEFA had met the previous afternoon, and after studying video footage from an alleged stamping incident at Elland Road, had banned Bowyer for three games. That meant he was out of the second leg. The timing could not have been worse or more provocative. Conspiracy theories abounded with many Leeds fans claiming UEFA didn't want an English side in the final. I wasn't so sure although the timing did strike me as particularly unfair on both Bowyer and Leeds. The bottom line is we were going into our biggest game in 26 years without one of our best players. Bowyer had scored six goals in the Champions League during the season, but now we had to do without him. It would prove a killer blow.

Bowyer's suspension remained the main talking point right up to kick-off, but I was feeling so nervous that I could hardly speak. I was so desperate to reach the final. It meant so much. Chances like this don't come along every year. After growing up watching us struggle against some very average sides in the old Second Division, seeing Leeds United play in a European Cup final would be the fulfilment of a dream.

The away seats were perched high in the corner of the third tier in the corner of the Mestella. Used for the host nation's three group games in the 1982 World Cup, Valencia have elaborate plans to extend the Mestella further from its current 53,000 to a phenomenal 74,000. Judging by the atmosphere inside the stadium for our visit, the Mestella is going to be an amazing place once the work is completed.

As the Leeds players emerged from the tunnel, they were met with a wall of noise. Valencia's Los Yumos were the first fan group to choreograph their support with colour cards, and the eye-catching effort for our visit showed they have not lost their touch. The hairs on the back of my neck were stood up so I dread to think what effect it was having on the 11 Leeds players out on the pitch.

We started okay only to fall behind to yet another 'hand of Sod'. Obviously inspired by Raul's efforts in the Bernabeu, Juan Sanchez flicked a Mendieta cross into the net with his hand. From the opposite end of the Mestella it was difficult to spot the offence, but watching television later, it was clear a hand had been used. I could be excused missing the offence due to the fact I was 150 yards away. The referee had no such excuse, but despite protests from several Leeds players, the goal stood.

We responded well, however, and had a great chance to draw level midway through the half when Mark Viduka created some space for himself on the left. He then chipped the ball perfectly for an on-rushing team-mate. This was a golden chance, but then I saw who was running on to the ball. David Batty.

Like all Leeds fans, I love Batts but he isn't a goalscorer. In his first spell with the club, he went five years without scoring. When he finally found the net at home to Manchester City in our Championship season, the celebrations on the Kop were worthy of winning the FA Cup. So when Viduka picked Batts out I knew the equaliser would not be arriving as he could only stab the ball tamely at the Valencia keeper.

Leeds continued to play well and the half-time whistle came at the wrong time for us because we were in control. Unfortunately, two quick goals after half-time for Sanchez and Mendieta meant the game was over. There was now no way back and as the home fans started to celebrate, we were left to reflect on the fact we wouldn't be going to Milan. I felt flat at us being on our way out, but I was still immensely proud of the team's efforts in Europe.

It had been an amazing nine months. We had been to some of the best stadia in the world and visited several new cities. There had been the emotion of a return to Istanbul and the dejection of Barcelona and that 4-0 defeat. But there had also been the joy of Milan, Brussels, Munich and Rome. Anyone who was inside the San Siro will also never forget the impromptu karaoke session involving fans and players as we celebrated reaching the second group phase. The tension of Deportivo as we clung to our aggregate lead is also something that will stay with me for a long, long time.

Alan Smith was sent off in stoppage time for a daft challenge and I wasn't the only Leeds fan relieved to hear the final whistle blown. The home fans celebrated inside the stadium before their team finally left the field. Around 30,000 then congregated behind the main stand, letting off fireworks and chanted for their heroes.

After the game, I wandered past this mass of fans and it was clear just how much the victory meant. I was gutted we were out, but if Leeds had to lose to any team then I am glad it was to Valencia. They had reached the final the previous season before losing to Real Madrid, but these Spanish fans were certainly not blasé about repeating that success. Long may that continue as well because there are few things I hate more in football than smug fans of a successful club. Manchester United fans spring most readily to mind although Liverpool, officially the world's best team again after winning three Cups in one season (according to the Scouse-loving media anyway) are running them close.

Walking back towards the city centre, we were treated to incessant horn-blowing from the passing cars as the home fans continued to celebrate. We saw one lad wearing a Leeds shirt who, obviously the worse for wear, was stumbling along the middle of the road with a bottle in his hand threatening passing cars. It turned out he'd been attacked outside the Mestella by home fans.

Understandably, he wasn't too happy but a couple of the lads persuaded him to come for a drink before he got himself hurt.

It turned into a good night. We were out of the Champions League, but a wake was not what was planned. Instead, I went out and celebrated what had been an enjoyable nine months. I had some wonderful memories.

Leeds' renaissance in European football has been superb for those of us able to follow the team abroad. For so long, it was an achievement in itself just to qualify for Europe. Before the last two seasons that had seen us reach the semi-finals of the UEFA Cup and Champions League, Leeds had enjoyed just three seasons in Europe out of a possible 20. In all three, we were knocked out in the second round. That has all changed now and although my bank manager may not agree, long may our success in Europe continue.

Leeds' Champions League adventure being over also brought sharply back into focus what was happening at home. I flew back to England the following day with a hangover. That probably didn't help my mood, but I couldn't help but think about my Dad. He had been staying at my Gran's house for the past couple of days and I was set to take him home on my return.

He had endured a miserable time since Christmas as the cancer left him in constant pain. Just moving around the house was a huge effort and I knew the end was not far away.

The Sunday before I flew to Valencia, we had managed to take Dad to Turf Moor for the Clarets' final game of the season. It had been planned with military efficiency with Burnley giving me special dispensation to drop Dad at the turnstiles. Walking any distance was out of the question. Peter, Dad's brother, then saved the parking space closest to Turf Moor for me so he wouldn't have far to walk after the game. I wasn't sure Dad would be able to sit through the whole game due to the pain, but he loved every minute.

Turf Moor has changed a lot in recent years, but it was where he had spent many of his happiest moments. Driving home after the game, he was like a different man. He was happy again. Not being able to watch football since Christmas had hit him hard, and for three or four days after our trip, he smiled through the pain. The drive home from Turf Moor saw Dad reminiscing about the days when Burnley were a genuine force in English football. I was so glad we had seen the Clarets in action one last time.

A little over two weeks later and his brave battle against cancer was over. I was glad Peter and I were with him at the end. Dad had been given an injection of morphine before we arrived at his bedside in the Keighley hospice, and although he looked to be sleeping, the nurse said the last thing to go would be his hearing. So we talked to him.

I told him my sister Caroline was on her way from her home in Wolverhampton to see him and I know he heard me because a small tear rolled down his left cheek shortly before 7am. Moments later he stopped breathing.

The man who had given me my love of football was gone. It was a moment I had been dreading for nearly two years since Dad had been diagnosed as having terminal cancer. The only consolation was that, at last, his suffering was over.

The summer was difficult. There were many bleak moments when the sadness threatened to become too much. The start of the football season in August was also difficult because it was a time of year we always looked forward to. To get me through, I focus on the many, many good times we had watching football and also the Leeds' Champions League adventure that helped me cope with the fear and dread that accompanied my Dad's decline.

And for supplying me with a much-needed thought diversion, I will always be grateful to David O'Leary and his Leeds United side for what they achieved in the 2000-01 season.

Also from Terrace Banter

Football books for those who know the score

Let There Be Light

Tony Gillan spent five years "lurking" behind the scenes at Sunderland's Stadium Of Light. The funniest football book you'll read this year (whatever year it is).   £10.00

Those Were The Days My Friends

Sleeping giants seem to be congregating in the First Division and this is one fan's view of what was a turbulent year on and off the pitch for Huddersfield Town.   £10.00

Tuesday Night In Grimsby

One man's story of his quest to travel the length and breadth of Britain to support his beloved Millwall. This is a true story of a masochist.   £8.99

An Englishman Abroad

The story of one man's fight for justice after being arrested and imprisoned during the 1998 World Cup. Martin Kerr's crime? He was wearing an England shirt.   £9.99

Invasion And Deportation

Two cousins, one a Darlington fan the other Arsenal, and their story of Euro 98. Forget the tabloid headlines - this is the reality for ordinary fans who follow England.   £8.99

St George In My Heart

When not on domestic duty with Millwall, Colin Johnson spent his time and money following his beloved England. And not as part of the official travel club either.   £10.00

We Fear No Foe!

The story of following Millwall over the last decade despite the nonsense Millwall fans have to face week in week out from the police, rival fans and the media. Not that all Millwall fans are angels . . .   £10.00

Bring Out Your Riot Gear - Hearts Are Here!

Welcome to an Edinburgh that doesn't exist in the tourist guides. An Edinburgh where youths fought each other over territory, style and football. The story of Hearts hooligans and Gorgie Aggro from 1981-86.   £8.99

All of the above books are available from all good bookshops (and some bad ones too) or direct from the publisher. Write for a full catalogue to Terrace Banter, PO Box 12, Lockerbie. DG11 3BW. Scotland or order online at www.terracebanter.com

About Terrace Banter

Terrace Banter was launched in October, 1998, as a football imprint of S.T. Publishing. Over the past decade football as a spectator sport has changed beyond all recognition, particularly for the ordinary fan. A great deal of working class culture and tradition is being cast to one side so that football can appeal to a new market, that of the "soccer fan".

Through Terrace Banter we hope to put down in print the experiences of the ordinary fan, warts and all, before they are lost forever in a sea of plastic seats and replica strips. Unless we document our own history, it is left to outsiders and the mass media to be judge and jury.

If you are writing or have written a football related book that you think would find a home at Terrace Banter, we'd be pleased to hear from you.

Terrace Banter
PO Box 12
Lockerbie
Dumfriesshire
DG11 3BW
Scotland

info@terracebanter.com